TELLING STORIES, SHARING CONFIDENCES

STORIES OF KINDNESS, HUMOR, AND OTHER MUSINGS, FOR UNCERTAIN TIMES

CAROL GEE

FRUITION
PUBLISHING
CONCIERGE SERVICES
FRUITIONPUBLISHING.COM
A DIVISION OF ALESHA BROWN, LLC

Telling Stories, Sharing Confidences: Stories of Kindness, Humor, And Other Musings, For Uncertain Times

© 2022 By Carol Gee

Published in Hampton, VA, by Fruition Publishing Concierge Services™. Fruition Publishing Concierge Services™ is a division of Alesha Brown, LLC.

Fruition Publishing Concierge Services™ can bring authors to your live event. For more information or to book an event, visit Fruition Publishing Concierge Services™ at:

www.FruitionPublishing.com

ISBN: 978-1-954486-39-3 Paperback

ISBN: 978-1-954486-40-9 eBook

Library Of Congress Control Number: 2022903543

DEDICATION

If I have learned anything from my life up to this point, it's that nothing demonstrates a person's true character like living a full life. That includes surviving disappointment and adversity. Even suffering the craziest situations, where I have frequently questioned, "What in the world was I thinking? Did I really just do that?" All serve as teachable moments showing that we are indeed human.

These fun stories of kindness, humor, and other thoughts are dedicated to men, women, and everyone everywhere. Hopefully, they will remind you that you are not alone no matter who you are or what you are going through.

My books are always dedicated to my husband Ronnie, who has always been my biggest supporter. He is also often my chauffeur and my "assistant," carrying my items and supplies wherever I go. Ronnie continues to be my beacon of light in good times and not-so-good times.

CONTENTS

FOREWORD

There are those who are distinguished and aspire to age gracefully. Then there is Author Carol Gee.

Somehow, this woman has managed to find humor in every inch of life, even during the worst times. I am always left in tears, hearty laughter, and asking, "No one could make this stuff up, but how could all of these things happen to the same person?" And just when you wonder what else could happen to top the last comical embarrassment, she serves it to you: funnier and twice as embarrassing as the previous occurrence.

Telling Stories, Sharing Confidences shares more of Author Carol Gee's private moments and the power of acts of kindness and community with a comedic twist. The many adversities and challenges Carol and her husband experienced often make people sad, bitter, and wondering why. Fortunately, Carol's humor and grateful spirit uplifts us all and demonstrates how to gracefully endure the journey called life.

In uncertain times and less than ideal life circumstances, *Telling Stories, Sharing Confidences* is the book we all need to lighten our burdens and warm our hearts. I recommend you read this alongside her other books and treat yourself to the gift of laughter. You'll quickly see why her books are referred to as "girlfriends' books because you will find yourself calling yours and sharing these funny stories. Laughter is better with friends.

Alesha Brown, The Joy Guru

Award-Winning Entrepreneur|Publisher|

Best-Selling Author

But those who hope in the Lord will renew their strength. They will soar on wings like eagles; they will run and not grow weary, they will walk and not be faint.

Isaiah 40:31, KJV[1]

---

1. The Holy Bible: King James Version. Dallas, TX: Brown Books Publishing, 2004.

KINDNESS

KINDNESS IN THE MILITARY

As an overly sheltered, 22-year-old woman entering the Air Force, I was lucky to have a wonderful supervisor on my first job after basic training and technical school. He took me under his wing and guided me through my first job with kindness and patience. With his guidance, I slowly blossomed.

His wife and kids also made me feel like I was a part of their family. Since he was a high-ranking member in the Masonic Lodge, invitations to their dances and other activities were also a given.

As the base was about fifty miles from the nearest big city—if you blinked, you missed the closest town—this much-appreciated act of kindness gave us something to do: a chance to dress up, dance, etc.

A couple of years ago, I pondered whether my first supervisor was still alive. After all, it had been over forty-seven years since we had last spoken. Googling him, I discovered that he was and still lived in Idaho, where the base was located.

Excited, I called him. He remembered me. At eighty-five years old, he sounded the way I remembered. His once gruff voice, while familiar, was now smoothed by years of smoking cigars (he kept spares in his socks) and sipping his beloved Jim Beam. The best part was that I got a chance to tell him how much he had meant to me and thank him for his kindness.

Idaho was where I also met Mrs. Hunter, director of the base's Recreation Center. Other than talking with me when I attended classes and other events at the Center, she did not really know me. Still, she invited me into her home to recuperate when I caught pneumonia, thinking that the barracks where I lived with the other female airmen probably wasn't the best place for me to recover.

In truth, her kindness showed me that "angels" did exist. Admiring her beautiful 'object de art' from her extensive travel worldwide, I also learned to appreciate the beauty of other cultures. As such, I couldn't wait to travel overseas.

Idaho was also where I met and married the love of my life. Indeed, his sweetness and kindness toward me when we dated led to my falling in love and marrying him. It has been his continued love and respect that has kept us united over the past forty-eight years.

"It is not the load that breaks you down.
It's the way you carry it."

Lena Horne, Singer

KINDNESS AT THE HOSPITAL

Over the past twenty-eight years, my husband has suffered one health crisis after another. As such, I feel blessed to still have him with me. Upper management for over twenty years at a well-known Atlanta Hospital until recently retiring, each time he has had a health crisis requiring surgery and hospitalization, I have taken him there.

Just the two of us with no family in the area, I needed to know that he had people (former staff, former colleagues) looking out for him whenever I could not be there. After his most recent surgery, and he was finally able to have visitors, both colleagues and staff stopped in to see him and me throughout his entire stay.

Not only visiting, they stopped by to see if we needed anything. This included the hospital CEO, whom Ronnie worked closely within his job capacity, who gave me a large number of tickets to pay for valet parking.

With Ronnie hospitalized for fourteen days, at eight dollars a day (sometimes I had to leave and come back), not only did paying for valet parking save us money, it relieved added stress during an already scary, stressful time.

Just Desserts

A retired Air Force veteran, my husband typically wears a baseball cap displaying his military status. Not long ago, on a trip, we decided to stop for lunch at a small mom-and-pop restaurant that we had noticed as we entered a small town.

While I stayed in the car, he went in to order a meal that we planned to eat once we checked into our hotel room. Noticing a favorite pie on the menu, he decided to purchase a slice for each of us. Quickly perusing the ticket before preparing to pay (something I often had to remind him to do), he noticed they had left one slice of pie off the ticket.

When he mentioned it, the owner who served him replied that the pie was on the house and thanked my husband for his service. Handing over his credit card to pay, he mentioned that I was in the car and that I, too, had served. The owner then re-rang the ticket removing the other slice also. We do not expect recognition for our military service, but it is nice when we receive it.

You Are Doing Fine!
You Got This!

Author Unknown

THE KINDNESS OF NEIGHBORS

This past year has taken a toll on us in numerous ways. I do not know about you, but there have been times while lamenting what I had lost (going out to lunch and dinner, gatherings with friends, traveling), I failed to acknowledge what I still had. One day, I sat down and jotted down the things I was grateful for.

For instance, throughout the height of the pandemic, one of my neighbors regularly checked on my husband and me. Either calling or texting, she reminded me that she was just down the street. She told us that she had to pass our house when entering and exiting our community, so she would not be going out of her way to stop by and drop off anything we needed.

The kindness of my neighbors began the day that we moved into our new home. As my husband and I took a brief break from unloading boxes, I glanced around the quiet, tree-lined community. I noticed a neighbor at the lovely house across and catty-corner from us was standing on her porch. Seeing me looking in her direction, she raised her hand to wave. After moving around the world for the past twenty years at that time, right then and there, I knew we were home.

This feeling of home was again present when my husband suffered the first of what would become many health episodes. Seeing the fire truck and ambulance, two neighbors across the street from us— one a Deputy Sheriff, the other a police officer— came over to see if there was anything that they could do.

As we had only just moved into the community and both worked, we had not met all of our neighbors, so that gesture meant a lot to me. Not knowing many people and having no family in the area, that kind gesture made me feel less alone. Indeed, the kindness of our neighbors has and continues to sustain me when life gets tough.

Storms Always Pass!

Even the most turbulent skies clear, and the sun
always reappears.

Night always gives way to daylight, and tomorrow is
always brand new.

Life is filled with these sustaining truths and more.

Truths like this:

You've got what it takes to get through anything you
are going through.

You do!

**Woman's World Magazine
5/4/20**[1]

---

1. "Storms Always Pass!" Women's World 4 May 2020. Print.

CAROL GEE

Love Thy Neighbor

For fifteen years or so, we lived across the street from our wonderful neighbor Bill and his wife. Over the years, we watched each other's homes when our families went on vacation, picked up the newspapers, mail, etc. We also periodically socialized.

A few years back, he started picking up our newspaper off the yard where the paperboy tossed it into the hedges and other areas and placing it on our front stoop where I could reach it without exiting my front door. My husband Ronnie would do the same if he got up and went to work before Bill did, or if Bill was not feeling well or took the occasional day off.

. . .

During Georgia's fickle temperature of infrequent snow and ice storms, my husband, a director in a local hospital's Food and Nutrition Department, was required to stay there to ensure meals were delivered to both patients and hospital staff, as many staff often were unable to report to work until the roads cleared.

Knowing that my husband was not at home, Bill would text me to let me know how the roads were if he could get out of his driveway and get to his job near the airport. Because I frequently used leave days instead of navigating icy roads, he would tell me not to get our mail out of fear that I might slip and fall. He would get ours when he got his.

A few years ago, Bill and his wife retired and moved out of state. The first morning I had to go outside to get the newspaper, a strong gust of wind blew cold air underneath my robe. I cursed Bill underneath my breath for moving. Naturally, I wished him and his wife well. However, due to his thoughtfulness and many kindnesses, I, for one, will never, ever forget him.

PAYING KINDNESS FORWARD

My earliest memory of a random act of kindness was when my second-grade teacher looked beyond the backward slant of my newly learned cursive writing to recognize the individual in me. The special attention she showed me went a long way in helping my self-esteem.

She also kept up with former students even after we had long left her classes. Seeing me in the hall one day, she asked if I was excited about the fifth-grade summer camp experience.

With tears flooding my eyes, I told her that my mother couldn't come up with all the funds before the deadline. So, her second act of kindness toward me was paying the balance of my summer camp registration (which my mother later repaid per their agreement).

Raised in the inner-city of Washington, DC, this teacher, who taught most of the second graders in the Adams-Morgan area, believed I would benefit from the fresh air and rural camp experience. And I did.

Throughout the week-long camping experience, I learned to recognize various plants and animals. I also learned to weave baskets out of select vines. I also listened to ghost stories around a campfire, etc.

Other times, I enjoyed the peace and quiet without the city noises of police sirens, fire engines, and other vehicles.

Periodically, I have been able to pay kindness forward. Such as when recently shopping at my local Walmart. As there were only two lanes open, I got into what appeared to be the shortest one.

With two customers ahead of me with a number of items each, I braced myself for the wait. As my turn grew closer, I glanced behind me to notice a man with what appeared to be a pair of shoes in a box in one hand and a pair of socks in the other.

In no real hurry, I asked if that was all he had. And, if so, if he wanted to go ahead of me. "That's very nice of you. Thank you," he said, getting in front of me and putting his items on the check-out counter.

A few minutes later, as I unloaded my items, I noticed a five-dollar bill on the items I had already unpacked. "The man ahead of you left that for you," the cashier said, looking at me quizzically.

"He only had two things, so I let him go ahead of me," I explained to her. I had not expected that, but it reminded me that kindness does pay.

Showing
Their Love

The best part of my nearly 30 years as an adjunct faculty member and university administrator (22 at Emory University) was my daily interactions and mentorship of the research assistants and other students working in various departments.

Every semester, we hired a number of students, and there was always one who needed me a little more than others.

The "more" included needing internships, assistance with foreign student visas, letters of recommendation, reviewing their resumes, etc.

"More" also included enjoying meals at my home during holidays when they either could not get home for the holidays due to bad weather, lack of funds, nowhere to go, or other reasons.

A few became more like family, even fondly calling themselves my "children." Not having children of my own, they regularly check on my husband and me, keeping me abreast of what's going on in their lives and frequently seeking advice.

During one of my chats with one of my "children," I mentioned that my husband was having surgery on one of his carotid arteries. As this was a tricky surgery, I was really scared.

On the day of my husband's surgery, two of them, one a busy public health analyst who today is more like my son rather than a former student, and another, an attorney, whose father I worked with when I was in the Air Force Reserves, and calls me her "god-mommy," took off from work to sit and wait with me.

Both only left once my husband was out of surgery and in recovery. In doing so, my "children" showed their kindness and love.

When times seems to stand still,
and you don't know what to do,
Just breathe in God's love and grace,
and on the exhale, breathe out fear.

Author Unknown

A Lasting Friendship

My husband and I, both young Air Force sergeants at the time, had just moved into our apartment at our brand new military base in South Carolina when I went to check the mail. Opening the mailbox, I immediately spotted the familiar brown envelope of a military check.

Seeing that the name on the check was not my husband's or mine, I took it to the apartment's leasing office. A couple of days later, there was a knock at our apartment door. There, a young woman about my age stood.

She introduced herself as the military officer's wife whose check I had returned. Thanking me for turning the check in, I invited her into our home. An hour later, I realized that I had just made my first friend at our new base.

Forty-six years later, our friendship remains intact despite our families being stationed in different locations worldwide during our twenty years of service. Over the years, I have realized that you do not have to call each other daily to sustain a friendship.

Today is a journey, and you're in the driver's seat.

Woman's World
2/1/21[1]

THE KINDNESS OF STRANGERS

Despite not feeling well, my husband, who has several health issues and often does not feel so well, insisted on going to Sam's Club with me. My goal was to quickly purchase the few items we needed so that I could get him home so that he could rest.

Remembering that we needed bottled water, before heading toward checkout, we headed to where the cases of bottled water were stacked.

As my husband bent to lift the first of three cases, two young men rushed over to us, saying, "Let us get this. This is too heavy for you to lift."

Putting the three cases we needed into our cart, we thanked them profusely for their kindness while marveling at the kindness of those nice, young men.

A Moment For You

You are a wonderful force in the world!

You probably don't take credit for it,
and you may not even notice it,
but you make someone's life better every single day.

With a smile, an encouraging word,
a strategic bit of advice,
a solution or two, or simply by being there.

You're someone powerful. You're you.

**Woman's World
9/28/2020**[1]

---

1. "A Moment For You." Women's World 28 September 2020.

   Print.

KINDNESS FROM A WONDERFUL STUDENT

We were fairly new to Atlanta. Without any family in the area, I prepared to wait alone in the hospital's family waiting room when my husband suffered a second heart attack, which required quadruple bi-pass surgery.

Responsible for the day-to-day operations at a well-known Atlanta university, looking up, I saw one of my research assistants, a young man I had grown quite fond of, approaching.

"I didn't want you to have to wait alone," he said, hugging me. Then, unpacking his backpack to study while we waited, he sat patiently with me until the procedure was over. Because of his kindness, I did not feel quite so scared and alone.

Twenty-eight years later (he recently reminded me how long we had known each other), we enjoy a sort of mother-and-son relationship, for which I daily count my blessings.

Kindness at the Local Post Office

Always having kindness bestowed upon me, I am excited whenever I can pay it forward. It happened recently while I was mailing several packages at my local post office.

As the line was growing long while the post mistress, who was working alone that day, weighed my packages to determine the postage, asked customers in line if anyone was there to simply purchase stamps or pick up a package, something that she could quickly handle.

The gentleman next in line replied that he only needed a stamp to mail a letter. Telling him the cost of the stamp, she asked if he had the exact change and prepared to sell him the stamp while I paid for my packages.

Stating he only had a ten-dollar bill, the postal worker told him that she was sorry, but that would take all of her change as the post office had just opened. The gentlemen said he would see if he had any change in his car, starting to leave.

Typically, tossing change in the bottom of my purse, I knew that I probably had the fifty-five cents he needed, and I offered it to him. Thanking me, he posted his letter and exited the post office.

A couple of minutes later, as I was heading to my car, I noticed two people in a van honking and waving at me. It was the gentleman from the post office and a lady I suspected was his wife. It appears they waited for me to come out of the post office so he could once again thank me for my kindness.

CAMPUS KINDNESS

Every semester as a university administrator, I hired both work-study students or research assistants to work with the faculty and me in my various campus departments. As their supervisor, I got to know them well while monitoring their schedules and job tasks such as library research for scholarly papers and other tasks to support research grants and other departmental needs.

Although each had their own workstation and computer, daily I could count on one of them working at the small; round work table in my office while I worked at my desk. During these times, they would talk to me, seek advice, etc.

One day, the young man I mentioned in earlier essays, whom I had grown quite fond of, shared that he did not know what he would do for food until he received his paycheck at the end of the week. Hearing this broke my heart.

Leaving home early the following day, I stopped by the grocery store near campus and purchased five-pound bags of potatoes, rice, and onions. I bought assorted condiments and spices and canned and fresh milk and meats.

In one bag, I also included several simple recipes that only required a few items to make a meal. I figured he could make this for dinner and perhaps take some for lunch, heating it in the small microwave I had bought for office use.

When he came into work that morning, I learned that he had one class. I told him to follow me to my car, where we transferred the groceries to his.

I told him to take them home and put them away. I then adjusted his work schedule to after his class that day so that he would not miss his work schedule. I simply could not bear the thought of him being hungry while trying to complete his degree.

My Neighbor Mowing My Grass, Relieved Me Of One Less Worry

The morning my husband was admitted to the hospital for quadruple heart bypass surgery, the guy who cuts our grass texted to say that he could not come cut our grass as scheduled as his mover was in the shop.

As it had been raining for several days, our grass had grown quite tall. Working a full-time job, spending the night before my husband's surgery at the hospital before going home to feed our cats and get some rest, at my husband's request, I was exhausted. The sight of the tall grass added more stress.

A couple of evenings later, as I was getting the mail, my lovely next door neighbor came over to say hello. I mentioned that my husband was in the hospital. And with my lawn man not available, I didn't know when I could get my grass cut.

A few hours later, I heard the sound of a lawnmower outside my house. Thinking it was my lawn man, imagine my surprise to see my neighbor cutting our grass. Thanking him profusely, I offered to pay him, but he refused to accept any money. Thanks to this wonderful neighbor, having my grass cut relieved me of one less worry at a really stressful time.

Animal Kindness

Growing up, we always had stray cats around our house; and my sister and I snuck food out of the house to feed them. So, I knew that I would get one when I got married and had my own home.

My husband was not a "cat person" when we got married. However, he probably decided that he was stuck with me and would probably be stuck with them as well.

While I also liked dogs, I realized early on that cats did well with my personality and often over-extended life, of going to school, working, and military relocations, both stateside and overseas.

My sister's military relocation was how I ended up with Muffin, a pretty long-haired, fluffy sweetheart, and Midnight, a black Persian mix (kitties with flat faces). Midnight was also a sweetie. Preparing for an assignment to Belgium, my sister asked if I would take them, knowing that I would.

Living in the Oklahoma City area at that time, she shipped them to me via Delta Airlines. Supposedly, I would only care for them for one year until she returned from her one-year European assignment.

Somehow, the time was never right (weather or cabin pressure issues) to reunite them at her new base, so I kept them. I loved and spoiled both for many years until Midnight succumbed to health issues.

Muffin became the "mother cat" when I adopted a cute orange-colored Morris (the famous cat) looka-like. Baby Tiger, who became known simply as "Baby," was also a stray that my sister fed alongside many strays that strolled past her apartment patio, the one time she and I were stationed in the same area.

Baby kept Muffin young. Toys that she had outgrown and hid under furniture were rediscovered and given a second life.

One such toy was a flat fish made out of a piece of carpet, which I had not seen or seen her play with for months.

Not feeling well one day, my husband came home from work early. An appointment with his doctor determined he had a kidney stone. In pain, waiting for it to pass, he stretched out on the daybed in the spare bedroom turned man-cave.

Eventually, he fell asleep. Only to wake up a few hours later to discover the flat fish toy on his pillow. Both Muffin and Baby (Muffin's shadow) were lying beside him, fast asleep. We suspected Muffin had decided that Ronnie was feeling poorly, and maybe a friend or two would help him feel better.

Showing Her Love And Appreciation

For nearly thirteen years, I had the pleasure of working for a brilliant physician/scientist. Although both she and my overall job were demanding, she constantly showed her appreciation for my efforts by showering me with gifts.

One time, it was a half-day at a local spa. Another time, it was a full spa day that included a full-body massage, having my hair done, my nails and feet done, and a healthy lunch.

Once, a massage therapist (another gift) that came to the house to do my treatment on my birthday really spoiled me. So much so that I cried when she moved out of state, leading me to try to find another one who did treatments at home.

Periodically, my supervisor would bring me back gifts from her extensive travel. An exotic looking dress from Trinidad, a necklace from another exotic location, and use of her timeshare for local trips and travels to exotic locales like Aruba and the Dominican Republic.

One especially lovely gift was a Lobster Gram. I had never even heard of something like that. Delivered by Fed-Ex, it contained two fresh Maine lobsters, two bibs, butter, spices, utensils to eat them with, and a pot to cook them in. She even made me take the day off to wait for delivery.

Luckily, my husband, who had spent nearly thirty years at that time working in food service, knew what to do. That evening, lobster accompanied by assorted veggies and a bottle of Merlot, given to me by another professor in my department, was a special dinner treat.

Eaten in my dining room, on my good china purchased when stationed in the Far East, complete with candles and soft jazz playing on the stereo, really elevated her lovely gift.

However, the highlight of the meal was my cat Phattious T Gee, or PhattyT, meowing and rolling on his back, hoping a morsel of lobster would fall his way. A fluffy, 18-pound bundle of fur, he provided "dinner theater."

Already giving 100 percent to my job and blessed to work for someone so appreciative, I constantly pondered how I could give even more.

A Moment For You

There is so much to believe in!

Believe that storm clouds always pass and clear sky
return: they do!

Believe in the sustaining power of love, hope, and
faith: They see us through!

Believe a beautiful future is headed your way: it's
true!

And absolutely believe in you!
There's no reason not to!

**Woman's World Magazine
6/15/2020**[1]

---

1. "A Moment For You." Women's World 15 June 2020. Print.

Kindness and Humor At 30,000 Feet

My husband's sweetness and kindness are what first attracted me to him. His beautiful, hazel eyes also did not hurt. So this particular incident should not have surprised me.

Years ago, when military members traveled, we were required to wear our dress blues. You know, the dark, blue jacket with all our military ribbons, badges, and other items, and matching dress blue skirt or slacks.

The two of us were on an airplane headed to my first overseas assignment to Okinawa. Somewhere between the east coast where we were vacationing with family and San Francisco, where we boarded the military plane for the long flight, I caught a slight cold. My nose felt stuffy, and I had a slight cough.

Hearing me sniffling while he was in the plane's restroom, my sweet man picked up what he thought was a small package of Kleenex.

So handsome in his dress blues, and with this in his hand, he walked down nearly half the plane to get to his seat next to me.

Turning to me, he said, "Here honey, I brought you this," handing me the small package. Shocked, I said, "What are you giving me this for?"

Startled by my response, he replied, "You were sniffing, so I bought these Kleenex."

Then, I noticed a military couple sitting across from us were leaning across their seat and watching our interaction.

Whispering, as not to be overheard, I replied, "Baby, this doesn't say Kleenex, it says Kotex." Judging by the look on his face, he was still confused, so I said, "This is what I use when Susie (what he nicknamed my lady part) gets sick."

Shocked and embarrassed, he too noticed the couple across from us still staring, probably wondering what I would do with my "gift." Glancing over the back of his seat, he noticed others also showing great interest.

As he had not tried to hide his gift, kissing him, I tucked the offending package in the pocket of the seat in front of me.

While this happened over forty years ago, I might not remember all the details. What I do remember is that Ronnie did not get up to go to the bathroom again until our layover in Guam before continuing our trip to Okinawa.

HUMOR

Good Morning

May the beauty of this new day
be a reminder of God's unconditional love for you.

Author Unknown

FALSE EYELASHES

I have a confession. I have never had much luck with (false stuff), you know, wigs, false eyelashes, fake fingernails, or anything that I was not born with. Did that stop me from trying them? Oh no!

For instance, one day, a military dorm mate suggested that my eyes would look good if I wore false eyelashes. Thinking why not, I allowed her to apply them to my eyes. I recall that she first ran a thin line of glue on the outer edge and pressed them one at a time on both eyelids.

Agreeing that my eyes did look good, she suggested that I wear my lashes to a party that night, which I did. At the party, the late R&B singer James Brown encouraged partiers to dance, which I did with gusto!

Just as I was getting down, (making it funky) as per the song and not from all the sweating, one of my false eyelashes came off, landing onto my lower lid. As James Brown screamed in his song, I also screamed, thinking a spider had landed on my eyelid. Oh God, Oh God! Help!

Leaving my cute partner on the dance floor, "sorry Dayquan, Quantay," (whatever), I ran to the restroom. There, I immediately removed the offending lash — where it remained stuck on my bottom lid. I also plucked the remaining one off, threw them both in the toilet, and flushed — twice!

After that experience, I simply decided to apply mascara to accent my eyes. Okay, if I am truthful, using too much made my eyes appear ringed by angry spiders.

Alas, I also discovered I was allergic to certain mascaras. As one time, my eyelids puffed up, and some of my eyelashes fell out.

Another time, I got eye makeup in my eye! Hey, do not act like this has never happened to you. Then, my eyes started to water, so I temporarily could not see.

One would have thought that I would have gotten the message the first few times I suffered makeup mishaps, but no! You know, if at first you do not succeed, try and try again.

HUMOR IS
CONTAGIOUS

To brighten my and others' day, I purposely find humor in daily living. It happened recently when I purchased some green spray paint from Walmart to paint a small bench in my backyard.

The bench was like those that appear on both sides of wooden picnic tables that my neighbor had put at the curb when they moved.

Gray in color and in great condition, I thought a coat of green paint would be perfect and make it a wonderful place to sit in my backyard to enjoy my flowers.

As I checked out at the register, the cashier asked for my ID. Presenting it, I asked why she needed it, as it was apparent I was a 'woman of a certain age.' She replied that some people sniffed spray paint to get high.

I told her that I was kind of clumsy, so people would know if I used it for that purpose. Knowing me, I would have green paint in my nostrils, eyebrows, hair, etc.

Picturing this, she burst out laughing, as did I. From now on, I suspect every time she sells spray paint to a customer, she pictures this and smiles.

JOB INTERVIEW

For as long as I can remember, I have always wanted a job where I could help people. Majoring in Sociology with a minor in Psychology as an undergrad, I had recently completed a Master's degree in Human Relations and Management when I learned of an opening at my local Division of Health and Human Services Division. So, I applied and was thrilled when I was called to interview.

My job interview appeared to be going well until the dreaded "Where do you see yourself in five years?" question.

As the position was for a social service 'generalist,' the next step was "specialist." I replied that "with a graduate degree and five years of demonstrated high performance with excellent evaluations, completed continuing education courses, etc. I expected to be promoted.

Interview prep always tells you to ask questions during an interview and show interest in the position you are applying for. Noticing my interviewer's nameplate read 'specialist,' I asked her how long she had worked there. She replied close to fourteen years.

I then asked how long it took her to be promoted. She replied that she had been promoted to her current position roughly six months earlier.

Boy, talk about opening your mouth and inserting your foot. Can you believe that I didn't get the job? Go figure!

WEARING MY SLACKS INSIDE/OUT

Except for periodically attending select administration meetings, most of my day as a department administrator at a well-known university was running the day-to-day operations.

This consisted of supervising staff, processing accounts payables, processing timesheets for my support staff and research assistants, and other duties kept me at my desk.

One day, as I got up from my desk, I noticed the deep seams that ran along the inside of my slacks were on the outside, indicating that I was wearing them inside out.

"Valerie, did you notice that I had my slacks on the inside out?" I asked my lovely administrative assistant, sitting at her desk outside my office. (Whenever I exited my office for coffee, I had to pass her to use the fax machine or the office copier).

While I loved all my employees, and they loved me (they frequently told others this), I knew that I sometimes got on their nerves with my tough stance on the ways things needed to be done (it's the military in me). So, I thought this was my assistant's subtle way of getting even.

"No, madam, I hadn't noticed." She replied. While happy I had not gotten on her bad side that day and that I had not had any meetings that day, I went to the restroom and put my slacks on the right way.

I don't mean to brag,
But, I can still wear the same earrings I wore in high
school.

Author Unknown

WHEN THE FUNK HITS THE FAN

When volume one of comedian Steve Harvey's book "Act Like A Woman, Think Like A Man" came out, two of my book club members and I went to the book store where he was appearing to purchase a copy.

While the three of us were standing in the super long line waiting to get our books, we plotted that when we got up to where Steve was, we would sing that little song from his old television show, The Steve Harvey show.

If you have never seen it, Steve's character played an inner-city school teacher. Before his teaching career, Steve's character had been part of a singing group with one hit song, "When The Funk Hits the Fan," which was actually a catchy tune.

To keep the long line moving, Steve Harvey's assistants had written our names on post-it notes for him to sign our books quickly. (I plan to steal that idea if I ever write a book that inspires extremely long lines).

When my two friends and I got to the counter where Steve sat, I said, "Hit it, girls!" and began to sing his song. Suddenly, I realized that I was the only one singing. What the heck? The other two had chickened out.

After signing my book, Steve looked at me and said, "Okay, run along now, Ms. Carol," with his typically deadpan look. (Translation: "Move it along, girlie, you holding up the line.") Thankfully, he did not say that out loud.

More than likely, he had that happen before, you know, someone singing that little ditty.

Still, can you believe my companions had the nerve to laugh after they had left me hanging? Okay, I admit it, I laughed too.

However, they can forget calling upon me "When the funk hits the fan," as it so often does in life.

TOE RINGS

After the false eyelash and fake fingernail debacles, where I noticed that one of the fake nails had come off as I was drying dishes and hoped it had not come off while I was cooking, you would think I'd learned my lesson. (You can read this story in my book "Random Notes.") From that day on, I swore off all "false beauty stuff."

That was until the day I saw a lady wearing a toe ring on what appeared to be a fresh pedicure. Thinking it looked cute on her, after having a pedicure, I decided that a toe ring would look cute on one of my toes also.

Purchasing a two-piece set from the Dollar Store, I went home to put one of them on. Bending down to put one on the second toe of my right foot, it immediately sprung off. Not a quitter, I tried again. The same thing happened!

Then I tried putting it on a different toe. It again sprang off. Alas, this time, one of my kitties chased it: the 18 pound, fluffy one. Whom promptly sat on it and offered a smug, cat-like grin. Toe ring caught and captured!

I finally tried on the other one to see if that would do the trick. It worked. Apparently, the first toe ring was too wide for my toe.

The next day, while running errands, I was told by a guy entering the grocery store that I had pretty feet. And that he loved my toe ring. Score!

You have so much potential and so many possibilities.

Woman's World Magazine
2/1/21[1]

"Mother Wit" and Wisdom

Growing up, my mother had sayings about *everything*. There was that warning about being prepared. I think. You know, "make sure you wear clean underwear in case you are ever in an accident." Frankly, if I had ever been in an accident, wearing clean underwear would have been the last thing on my mind.

There was also what I called "the value of condiments." You know, "You'll catch more flies with honey than with vinegar." Good to know, if I ever wanted to catch flies, that is (which I didn't at the time, and still don't).

Then, there was the wisdom of loyalty. Or maybe it was choosing friends who weren't crazy. I wasn't quite sure of the lesson there. You know, "If Susie jumps off a bridge, are you going to jump too?" Okay, I am loyal, not crazy like Susie, as it appears.

Even back then, there was a lesson about conservation, or maybe it was about going green. "Shut that door behind you. You are letting flies in. What is wrong with you? People would think that you were raised in a barn."

If this was not enough, we were bombarded with new words, frequent threats, and quite often fear.

- *Stamina:* "You will sit there until you eat that spinach, egg salad, etc., Missy."
- *Promises* (accompanied by fear): "You will understand when you get to be my age."
- *Fear (again)*: "Just you wait. One day you will have children, and they'll turn out just like you."
- *Fear* (yet again*) and Guilt*: "I'm not always going to be here, and you will be sorry you acted like this when I'm gone." (How do you know? I always thought this to myself because I didn't dare talk back.)

And, let us not forget the proper way to end a conversation. "Because I said so."

SETTING MY MENU
ON FIRE

To celebrate our forty-second anniversary, I selected a lovely French bistro where I had enjoyed lunch with friends numerous times. The food and service were always good.

My husband had never been there, so I thought he would enjoy it. Dinner service was comprised of tables with white table cloths and candles on the tables. They also had set up a small stage where musicians played French tunes.

Perusing the unusually long, laminated menu, I asked my husband, "Do you smell something burning?" At that exact moment, I noticed that my menu had caught on fire by the small tea light candle in the center of the table.

Making my selection, I handed the menu with a small hole burned right in the center at the top to the waitress. Although she pretended not to notice, my face was red. Causing my husband to joke that he couldn't "take me anywhere."

THE "CHANGE"

Frankly, I never asked for "the change." I asked for Scotch and lots of steamy sex, if I am not mistaken. Admittedly, it is hard to feel sexy when sweating like a pig both day and night.

Growing up, I had often overheard the women in my mother's beauty shop talking about "the change." As kids take things literally, I remember watching the woman I heard was going through it whenever she came to get her hair done. I often wondered what she would "change" into.

I secretly hoped she would change into a puppy so I could play with it, as we had cats, and my mother would not allow us to have a dog. (A stray dog did show up some years later, and she changed her mind, but I digress.) After all, in my childlike mind, if you could not change into something fun, why bother?

Alas, the only thing I noticed was the woman always seemed to be sweating and constantly wiping her face with her powder puff. I also noticed the streaks of makeup left on her face from the constant wiping. Nothing else interesting happened as far as I could tell.

My nine-year-old self resolved to never go through "the change." The old cliché "never say never" is true. I eventually went through "the change," which included hot flashes in the daytime and night sweats. I was also dry in places that should have been moist.

Despite all the above, I consider myself lucky. I never had mood swings, anger, or other issues I heard others say they suffered.

And my husband was very agreeable. After the first two nights where I flung off the bed covers along with my nightshirt, he realized that he was not going to "get lucky" and rolled over in the bed and began snoring.

Thankfully, nothing lasts forever. Over the years, most of my menopause issues have all but disappeared. I don't know who was happier, my husband or me.

BAGEL DAY

Once a month, on Wednesdays, the school at the university where I worked offered bagels, orange juice, and coffee as a way for students, faculty, and staff to mingle and get acquainted.

Typically, staff would get their food and go back to their offices. I, however, would stop briefly and chat with students and professors whom I knew before heading back to my office.

On one particular Wednesday, I wore a new, pretty mango-colored blouse that I had recently bought. Loving how the color accented my face and skin tone, you could not tell me that I was not cute.

Sipping my juice, I accidentally spilled some down the front of my new blouse. Hurriedly dabbing at it with water, I removed most of the stain. For a while, all that remained was a huge, wet spot that garnered numerous responses from co-workers.

"What happened?" One of my co-workers asked, pointing to my blouse. Then one after another asked the same question. Tired of answering these inquiries, I remained in my office until the spot dried.

Humor At The Cancer Clinic

Typically, a cancer diagnosis does not inspire much humor. During the first three weeks of the eight weeks of radiation treatment my husband underwent, he and I had both been under a lot of stress, although we tried to keep it hidden.

My husband being a quiet man, hiding stress was easier for him than for me. Any stress and fear that I felt, I tried to keep hidden so he would not worry about me while he was undergoing his varied health issues.

As my husband's treatments were located in the tunnel of the local cancer center, we had to use one of three elevators to reach it. Typically, I tried to stand in the middle to reach either the first or the last elevator before the doors closed.

One day, with the arrival of the elevator furthest way, I rushed to get on before the door closed. As my husband always let women and the elderly get on before him, I waited for him to get on. Suddenly, the elevator door shut, and he had not got on.

It turns out I had gotten on the elevator going *up* instead of the one going down. Getting off on the first floor, I immediately pressed the down elevator to the tunnel where my husband was waiting for me.

"Didn't you hear me ask where you were going?" He asked, looking at me oddly. Obviously, not! On the first floor, I encountered a hospital volunteer with a cart full of assorted snacks, who offered me one, which I held up to show him.

Although it was not that funny, we both laughed hysterically. I realized that we both needed the laugh. In doing so, I felt some of the tension that I had been carrying ever since my husband's cancer diagnosis and treatment began to leave my body.

When time seems to stand still,
and you don't know what to do,
Just breathe in God's love and grace,
and on the exhale, breathe out fear.

Author Unknown

Making A Fashion Statement

If I like them and the price is right, I have been known to purchase the same style of shoes, earrings, or bangles in multiple colors. With a particularly busy morning, around two o'clock in the afternoon, I finally decided to take a break.

Checking my makeup in the ladies' room mirror and turning my head, I noticed that I was wearing two different colored earrings. Although they were the same style, one was in solid gold, the other was black and gold.

"Did you notice that I had on two different color earrings?" I asked my office assistant, who was known for his fashion sense.

"Yes," he said, "however, I thought you were making a fashion statement since they matched your gold blouse and black slacks." See? I was making a fashion statement and did not even know it.

Lost In A Store Parking Lot

I admit that I am directionally challenged. I am known for losing my car in store parking lots. So I was relieved when I spotted my car recently after exiting a store.

Approaching it, I pressed the key fob to open my car door. Nothing happened. So, I pressed it a second time. Again, nothing happened.

Suddenly, a man's voice behind me said: "Excuse me, but that's my car." To prove it, he pressed his key fob. The door opened, and he got in.

Confused, I backed up to notice the tail end of a car the same color and model as mine, blocked by a large black SUV.

Approaching it and unloading my items into the trunk, a voice behind me said: "I see you found your car." It was the owner of the other vehicle.

"Yes, I did," I replied, attempting a smile. But, I admit, I felt a little silly.

Getting Gas

Since retiring and working for myself, plus with the onset of the pandemic, I don't need gas as often as I did when working a full-time job.

Subsequently, I noticed my need to refuel recently while running errands. (I try not to get below a quarter of a tank).

Nearing a station I frequently used, I pulled over. There, I paid for my gas and bought lottery tickets and scratchers.

Back at my car, I released the latch to open the gas tank. Nothing happened. I lifted it a second time, again nothing. Frustrated, I thought I needed to take my car to the Toyota dealership to see what was going on with my gas cap latch.

Back home, and about to enter my house from my garage, I noticed that the hood of my car was raised. The latch I had pulled earlier? That was the hood latch, not the gas cap latch! I promise you, I cannot make this stuff up.

REPLY ALL

I had been in my new position on a well-known Atlanta university campus for two days when the trainer from the Tech Support department emailed me to schedule training on the school's email and other computer systems.

While I worked on the same campus at two other schools for close to thirteen years, each school used a different email system for both internal and external communications.

I immediately confirmed a date and time. A few minutes later, the trainer emailed me that I had hit "reply all" when confirming. Everyone—students, staff, and professors—had received my response.

While no harm was done—thank goodness it had not been something that should have been confidential—boy, did I feel silly.

The world told her to be invisible.
She heard *be invincible*.

Unknown

SENIOR DISCOUNT

Thursday is Senior Citizen day at my local thrift store, and everything is 20 percent off. They also have a military and veteran's day discount for which I am eligible.

Spotting a pretty china teacup that reminded me of those on Downton Abbey for only eighty-nine cents, I took it to the check-out counter. "I would like my senior discount, please," I said to the cashier.

I recalled my late father used to remind vendors of this discount, and I had often felt frustrated as this discount was so small. However, as I have gotten older, I find myself requesting it and any other discounts for which I am eligible.

"I'm sorry, the senior discount is only available on Thursdays," the cashier remarked. "Today is Wednesday, however, eighty-nine cents is already a bargain for such a lovely cup," she continued.

I agreed, however, I felt my face getting red. Then I thought, you cannot fault a girl for trying to save money.

Business Card

I had just finished a productive business meeting to discuss writing a case study for a professor at my former university.

This professor was a retired Army General, and as I too was a retired military veteran, had written several cases that had been taught in the classrooms before retiring. As I was also recommended by a former professor in my old department, who felt that I was a good fit to research and write the case, I felt confident about my chances.

Preparing to leave, I handed the person whom I had just met with what I thought was my business card. Glancing at it, he smiled and handed it back to me.

Saying, "You probably want this back." Puzzled, I reached for it and noticed I had handed him my lottery scratch-off. (In my defense, it was the same size as my business card).

As I had scratched off $5.00, yes, I did need it back, so I swapped it for my actual business card. (If you read my other books, you will realize that I am not making this stuff up. Welcome to my life!)

Drive Carefully As Buffalo Are Dangerous

While this happened many years ago, I still remember it as if it were yesterday. A two-military service-member couple at the time, we were driving to our new Air Force base in Rapid City, South Dakota. While my husband drove, I typically read the map (this was before GPS).

As we had been on the road most of the day, it was about four o'clock when we found ourselves entering a large park. Rounding a corner, we came across a sign that read, "Drive carefully as buffalo are dangerous." Say what? I thought.

Suddenly, a huge herd of wooly buffalo was right in front of us. "Did the map say anything about buffalo?" My husband asked. Realizing that he was being sarcastic, I replied, "no."

Keeping our eyes on these woolly beasts, we drove carefully toward an area with picnic benches where we stopped to glance at the map. Determining that we were less than an hour from where we needed to be, I was relieved.

All the while, I was secretly praying that the 'deer and the antelope' would not also decide to come out to play before we found our way out of this huge park. Years later, we took my mom to that same park when she visited. As I recalled, she was fascinated by the park and the buffalo, which she had never seen before. I could relate.

HEALTH FOOD

One day, a co-worker suggested we try a new health food place that had recently opened close to where we worked. The next day we did.

Entering the building, we noticed a small table near the door, offering healthy snacks to sample. My co-worker poured air-popped corn, dried fruits, and assorted nuts into her hand using the small spoon provided.

Growing up, I have always been considered prissy, and folks still think I am. So, thinking how uncouth this was to pour the items into her hand, I chose one of the small plates nearby, spooning some of the same things in it.

Turning to walk away, my co-worker said, "You might want to leave that lid behind so they can recover the snacks."

It appears my "plate" was actually the lid to one of the snack containers. Dumping the snacks into my hand, I hurriedly put the lid back on the table and scurried away.

Drink Plenty Fluids, And Call Me In The Morning

Feeling unwell the morning after celebrating my promotion to "sergeant" in the Air Force, I thought the festivities had gotten to me the night before. Calling in sick, I figured a day of rest would help me feel better.

Still feeling unwell the next morning, I went to see the base doctor. It turns out I had the flu. "Go home, get some rest," the doctor said. "And drink plenty of fluids," he added.

I called my supervisor and repeated what the doctor said. Later that evening, as I sat at the bar at the NCO (Non-Commissioned Officer's) club, I happened to look up to see my supervisor entering.

Surprised to see me, he asked, "What are you doing here? You are supposed to be sick and resting in your barracks."

"Well, the doctor told me to drink plenty of fluids. I did not have any in my barracks, so I came here." I replied, hoisting my glass of orange juice...with a shot of gin for him to see.

"If they hadn't told me that I was ugly,
I never would have searched for my beauty.
If they hadn't tried to break me down,
I wouldn't know that I am unbreakable."

Gabourey Sidibe, American Actress

(Movie, Precious, Series, Empire, etc.)

OTHER MUSINGS

Octopus Tempura, Etc.

During the past few months, I have found myself indulging in memories, recalling several informative years, numerous adventures, and experiences. Many of these go way back when I was much younger and served in the Air Force.

Like the three years Ronnie and I lived in Okinawa, Japan. One of these memories was when a young airman whom I supervised offered me what he said was some *type of fish*.

Cooked a crispy, brown color in a batter known as tempura, I selected a small piece. Popping it into my mouth, I chewed, and chewed, and chewed it. The more I chewed it, the meat appeared to get bigger versus smaller.

"What kind of fish is this?" I asked. "It is kind of tough."

"Oh, my bad. That is actually Octopus deep-fried in a tempura batter."

Although it did not taste bad, the thought of those eight-limbed things with bumps made it difficult for me to swallow. Since we all worked at a console with cubby holes, I kept tissues or paper towels handy to wipe up spills. Discretely, spitting the octopus piece into a paper towel, I balled it up and threw it away.

"What did you think? Did you like it?" He asked, all innocent-like. He had no idea how close he came to my ordering him to "drop-down and give me fifty push-ups" right then and there.

Instead, I made sure he took a large amount of parts requests the rest of the day while I worked on other tasks. Even though I was the base's Supplies shift supervisor, I frequently stepped in and took supplies and parts requests when the department got super busy.

However, a lesson learned: from that day on, I made sure that I knew what I was eating before accepting it (like the candy made of rum where the label read

RUM in English). Yes, I would like a few of those, please, and thank you.

Everybody Has A Story

I am an adoring wife, a loving sister, aunt, cousin, friend, mentor, book author, and business owner. These are just some of the things most people know about me. I am also a diabetic and a mini-stroke survivor. All are part and parcel of what makes me, well, me.

When people learn that I served in the Air Force, they say I don't look like a soldier (airman). "You look too soft, too feminine looking," they say.

I have always taken that to mean that I did not fit their idea of what a female service person looked like. You know, the "hard looking I can shoot a gnat at fifty paces" kind of woman. (Actually, I earned a military marksmanship ribbon, thank you very much.)

My love of perfume and all things girlie aside, I am pretty tough. Indeed, life has demanded that I be. After all, few people have the fortitude to spend six weeks on their hands and knees cleaning grout from bathroom tiles with a toothbrush (military basic training). Or once eaten octopus tempura in Okinawa, Japan, and lived to tell about it.

Subsequently, the military guided my life's trajectory, affording me an education, opportunities to travel, and to learn about other people and cultures.

Few know that growing up, I dreamed of writing the 'great American novel,' starting with writing little short stories to entertain my younger sister. Poems followed.

Two, *"Ode To That Lying Scum"* and *"Swinging From Chandeliers, Do You Suppose The Warranty Covers That?"* came about after dates with "Mr. Wrong" followed by "Mr. Crazy," (He really *was* crazy if he thought I was doing *that* on the first date! Besides, I did not, and still do not care for heights.

I am proud to say that I eventually wrote and published my debut book, *The Venus Chronicles*, followed by a robust freelance writing career. Four books later, and by retaining faith in my dreams, I finally did it. I became a writer!

To paraphrase a quote from the 1948 police drama *The Naked City*: "There are eight million stories in the naked city. This is mine."

COLONOSCOPY

A colonoscopy is just one of the age-generated health procedures we need as we grow older and is designed to check —well — our colons. While most of us do not often think about our colons unless we have some kind of issue, they can develop tumorous growths that can become cancerous. Colon cancer is now the third most common type of cancer in the United States.

So when my doctor told me it was time for mine, I made an appointment for the procedure. Alas, there is a lot of "prep" before the procedure. While different doctors prescribe different prep procedures to clean out the colon before the procedure, this doctor prescribed an enema, a liquid medicine inserted into the rectum.

Not all that graceful to start with, I pondered the best way to insert the medicine. I pooh-poohed (pun intended) lying on the bed for fear I would get it wet. Finally, laying down on the floor in the master bedroom seemed the best way.

As I started to insert the first medicine vial, I glanced up to see both of my kitties staring at me. They had been somewhere else in the house earlier. If they could have talked, I imagined one asking, "What the heck is she doing?"

"I don't know," I imagined the other one would reply, "but if she tries to sniff our butts, I am so out of here." (Something animals do for some unknown reason).

"I hear you," the other one would reply. The nerve of them! After all, they sniff each other butts, and now I am the weirdo?

Today, both kitties have long since joined other beloved pets "over the rainbow bridge." Both lived fourteen to almost seventeen years before illnesses took them away.

Today, dealing with my husband's fragile health, my heart cannot deal with the possibility of losing anything else I love.

I have another colonoscopy appointment coming up next month. As I prep for it, and those that follow, I will never forget them and how much love the two of them gave me with great fondness and much laughter.

Necessity Is Often The Mother Of Invention

I typically wear tops and blouses with sleeves to my elbows or longer that cover my arm flab. However, one day, I decided to risk exposing my arm flab for looking *cute*.

The morning started fine. Every time I glanced at myself wearing my cute top, I felt good.

You know the old saying, "If you think you look good, you often feel good." All this changed around two o'clock that afternoon when the temperature in my office dropped drastically (I later learned the AC malfunctioned), and I still had three hours to go before getting off of work.

I was freezing. Even my goosebumps had goosebumps. Knowing that I could not make it three more hours sitting in front of my computer with my arms folded for warmth, I frantically looked around for something—anything—to put on.

Spotting a decorative cloth wall hanging I had made to decorate my office space, I snatched it off the wall and flung it around my shoulders.

Similar to those sporting the names or initials of colleges, the wall hanging was roughly about 36 inches long and 12 inches across. The pointed end of the cloth sported a tassel the same color as the rest of the material.

Unfortunately, my wall hanging only covered one shoulder and only a part of the other arm. Thus, I had to hold it in place with one hand to keep it around me. This resulted in a hunting and pecking motion of the keyboard with my right hand.

This went on for maybe an hour or so when suddenly I looked up to see one of the technicians from our IT department standing at my desk with a puzzled look on her face.

I figured my weird typing must have made her think I had a computer problem. (Call me paranoid, but I have always believed that companies could watch what workers did with company computers).

"I like your shawl," my co-worker said, pointing to my banner/shawl. I burst out laughing, which must have really made her think that I was crazy and could not type.

Incidentally, the mauve and wine colors of the banner complimented the hot pink blouse that I had on, so I could see how she thought it was part of my outfit. I explained what it was and why I was wearing — well — a wall hanging.

As much as I have always hated to admit it, mother was right! Necessity is often the mother of invention.

MURPHY'S LAW

Is it just me? That every time we women think that we've "got it going on," that something will happen that shuts that thought down?

For example, there was the time I was wearing a pair of black slacks that fitted me just right. You know, they caressed my hips and thighs just so. I was so in love with the way I looked and felt that nobody could tell me a thing.

Suddenly, I felt something touching my leg. Thinking it was a bug or something, I started shaking my leg, trying to get it off. Imagine my relief and embarrassment to discover that it was only a dryer sheet which, by that time, was peeking out from beneath my pant leg.

My relief soon turned into horror when I noticed a rather *fine* man giving me the eye, alas, not for the reason I wanted him to. In fact, he looked amused as he watched me shaking my leg, much like a dog does after peeing! Oh well, I am a married woman, so I shouldn't care that he was looking at me. (However, I did.)

Indeed, my run-ins with Murphy's Law are legendary. Take the morning that I was innocently nibbling a toasted bagel with jelly.

Suddenly, a tiny drop of jelly fell on the mango blouse I was wearing (the one that I thought made my face glow). Fortunately, my breasts were there to catch it or, who knows where the jelly would have ended up?

Cleaning the jelly stain off as well as I could, it still felt like it was hugely visible. Naturally, this was the day my god-daughter invited me to her going away luncheon.

At lunch, we celebrated her realization that practicing criminal law was no longer the kind she wanted to practice and accepting a new legal spe-cialty. Well, at the luncheon, I spilled water on my blouse. Was the jelly lonely? I pondered.

Murphy's Law is the grand equalizer, as no woman is immune. For instance, the woman sitting to my left spilled food on herself.

Then, the lady to my right spilled something that landed on her eyeglasses that dangled from a chain around her neck. However, she looked peeved when someone pointed that out to her. (Perhaps she had planned to have it for a snack later)?

By the end of the meal, all of us, except for the lady who had wanted to save her tidbit for later and still appeared peeved, decided to form a club for women who should never leave home without a bib and were not ashamed to admit it.

Another time, one of my co-workers discovered she had on two different shoes. They were the same color but in a different style. Naturally, as Murphy's Law would have it, she did not notice this until she arrived at work. This was also the day she had worn a scarf to match her outfit, so you know she thought she; had it "going on."

For the most part, these things are harmless, although embarrassing. My confident side tries to take them in stride. My cynical side, however, thinks it is some kind of conspiracy dreamed up by men. I try to tune it out by eating cookies.

Wouldn't you know that one of the cookies crumbled? And a few of the crumbs slid down the neck of my blouse?

WHERE ARE YOU FROM?

(What I Called Seeking Common Ground, Others Find Alienating.)

"Who was that?" my sister asked one day as we met for lunch. She was talking about the lady I was speaking with as she approached.

"Oh, she thought I was someone else," I answered.

"The way you and she were talking and laughing, I thought you knew her." My sister remarked.

What can I say? I am a people person. I have always been fascinated with people: what made them tick; what made them do the things they did. This curiosity led me to major in sociology and minor in psychology as an undergrad.

In graduate school, I figured courses in human relations would further enhance my understanding of the human condition. Upon graduating, a short stint as a mental health counselor afforded further insight.

As an active-duty airman, I fully embraced the people and culture of all the places I lived. I sampled local cuisines. I even took classes to learn to make some of the exotic dishes.

So imagine my surprise when I learned that I was hurting others by uttering these four simple words, "Where are you from?"

Some years back, this topic of asking folks where they were from was part of a study about Race in America, which appeared in the Sunday edition of my hometown newspaper, the Atlanta Journal-Constitution.

According to the article, when individuals who appeared to be from other countries were asked, "Where are you from?" many were offended. They assumed the person asking did not think they were American when many were born in the U.S.

My asking individuals where they were from is not about making individuals feel like an outsider, as the article indicated, but my way of trying to find some common ground as we transacted business together.

For instance, while serving in Okinawa, I vacationed in Seoul, South Korea, for a week. This was where I learned the sales lady at my neighborhood beauty supply store was from when I asked.

I shared that I once visited there while serving in the military. She seemed surprised when I mentioned I liked Kimchi, a pungent, fermented cabbage dish. Not so much when I said I also loved Bulgogi, a delicious marinated beef steak.

Another time, I asked the lady in front of me in Publix if she was from Panama when I noticed she was wearing a Mola (an embroidered fabric from that country) on her blouse. "Yes," she answered. "How did you know?"

I shared that my husband, also a retired vet, and I had enjoyed a three-year assignment there. I also shared that I found Panama to be a lovely place to live; that the people were warm and friendly, which seemed to please her.

People frequently ask where I am from. They say they detect an accent but are unsure where it is from. I tell them that I was born in Virginia and raised in Washington, DC. Having lived practically all over the world while serving in the military, any accent detected was part and parcel of the various locales.

Am I offended by their asking? Not at all. After all, I am the product of Southerners who frequently asked newcomers where they were from. Or "who were their people?" I suspected this was to establish whether the newcomer was related to them or someone they knew.

So, the thought that my innocent question might be alienating gives me pause. Instead of asking another beauty supply sales lady where she was from, I ask, "Hon, do you carry Gonesh (a delightful brand of incense I have enjoyed for over 40 years).

Gonesh is typically identified by numbers. You know, Number 4 rather than its name Perfumes of Orchards and Vines. While unbeknownst to me, she probably wondered how I knew her name was Hon?

COFFEE, MEMORIES, AND FRIENDSHIP

As I waited for my coffee to finish brewing, I pondered which coffee mug to choose, looking at the selection hanging in my sunny, yellow kitchen. Would it be the one from Myrtle Beach, South Carolina, a thank-you gift from my wonderful cross-the-street neighbors for watching their home, getting the newspaper and the mail while they went on vacation?

Contemplating this particular mug reminded me of the year my husband and I, both Air Force sergeants at that time, were stationed there.

As there was a wait for a two-bedroom house on the base, we rented an apartment in the nearby city of Conway. While taking a back way to the base only took roughly fifteen minutes, I longed to be closer to the beach.

My wish was granted when an Air Force Major whom my husband worked with at the base hospital told him that the house across the street from her was for rent. And only one mile from the beach.

Further conversation with the Major revealed that, based on her recommendation, the owners were interested in renting to us with one caveat: we would take good care of their home.

To ascertain the type of renters we would make—you know, were we slobs or druggies (yes, there is frequently drug use in the military)—they visited us with roughly ten minutes' notice at our Conway apartment.

We knew we passed their test when they told us how much the rent would be, which was much less than I ever imagined.

Thus, the wife's sister became our landlord when the owners moved out of state. What began as a renter and landlord relationship became a friendship that spanned over three decades until her passing.

Another morning, my mug of choice was from a set that our neighbors brought back from visiting Charleston, South Carolina. Painted on it were the yellow, blue, and orange houses along the Battery, known as Rainbow Row. Their colorful facades delighted my senses every time I saw them.

Selecting the Charleston mug, my mind flashed back to the sights, sounds, and smells of Charleston's City Market. The local ladies weaving baskets from marsh grass, a locally harvested vine, are a treasured memory. I can see their nimble fingers working fast as they created those beauties.

Memories of having lunch at one of the many nearby restaurants were capped off by a scoop or two of homemade ice cream at one of the ice cream shops.

Through the years, our gift mugs included two with handles shaped like guitars from our friends' Nashville trip. Cobalt blue mugs were souvenirs from their visit to Virginia's Busch Gardens amusement park.

Like most professional couples, we do not socialize as much as we would like. There is the occasional cookout or annual Christmas gift exchange showing our appreciation of one another.

Subsequently, when reaching for one of my mugs, I am reminded that something as simple as sipping my morning coffee from a cup gifted from wonderful neighbors not only evokes fond memories but often creates lasting friendships.

Serving My Country, In Turn, Saved Me

I remember it as if it were yesterday, when my mother retired from her civil service job in Washington, DC, and announced that we were moving back to her small, Virginia hometown. Lying in my bed that night and looking up at the ceiling, I wondered how it happened that I'd be entering the twelfth grade in a new school.

Being the new girl in my senior class was hard. Although the girls were standoffish, the boys were too friendly for my or the other girls' liking.

As if living in a small town where I did not know many people was not bad enough, graduating, and working a dead-end job, day after day, my life seemed desolate.

One day, flipping through a magazine in the breakroom of the shoe factory where I worked, there was an ad for the Air Force. Seeing a young, African American woman in her crisp, blue uniform, sitting in front of a console with numerous knobs and gages, I knew this was my answer.

Grabbing an ink pen, I tore out the prepaid card and filled it out. Dropping it in a mailbox on the way home, I completely forgot about it. That is until the day an Air Force recruiter called me.

"Carol, telephone!" My younger sister yelled. "It's some sergeant!"

"Who is this sergeant?" My mother asked in a voice steeped in suspicion. "What have you done?" She asked as if thinking it was the police, and, horror of horrors, I was on my way to jail.

I wanted to tell her that I did not think the police called before coming to arrest a person, but knowing she did not possess a sense of humor, I remained quiet.

The recruiter brought the military entrance exam to our house three days later. Before I knew it, I was on an airplane bound for military basic training in San Antonio, Texas. I was 20 years old.

"Put out that cigarette," barked the drill sergeant to a guy who had just lit up. With his crisp uniform and straight military bearing, he brooked no argument.

"All of you pick up your baggage and form a single line!" The sergeant continued to bark. Oh man, Carol, you have done some stupid things in your life, but this is the stupidest thing you have ever done, I thought to myself. Still, there was no turning back now. I'd opened Pandora's Box, and all manner of stuff was destined to come flying out.

"I am an American Airman," the Air Force creed began. This was both "a promise to the country and its colleagues." The promise, however, did not mention that I would spend six weeks on my hands and knees cleaning grout from restroom tiles—with a toothbrush. Nor did it mention I would spend six weeks sleeping on the cold floor.

Initially, this was to save time each morning. Secondly, it was not to mess up my military bunk after finally learning how to make it, where the sergeant bounced a quarter on it to test its tight, four-cornered facade.

After all, there was no way I could make it up, shower, dress, eat and be in formation on time. Other women did similar things, including sleeping partially clothed at night to get a head start.

Lined up according to height, we marched everywhere in formation. "Forward, march! Hut, two, three, four," called out the drill sergeant as we marched across the base compound.

Marching in my size five combat boots (the smallest standard-issue available), my voice rang out with the others:

"Over hill, over dale, as we hit the dusty trail, as the Caissons go rolling along." Despite the physical demands of basic training, surprisingly, I thrived.

When I entered the Air Force, there were only a handful of women. We were part of a new breed of airmen, albeit with breasts. We did not seem to fit what people thought military females looked like or how they acted. This allowed me to set my own standard of a military woman and what she could do.

It is no exaggeration to say that the military changed my life. It was not until then that I discovered what a truly sheltered young woman I had been.

For instance, in my squadron, I found many women did not have the same basic value system that had always been instilled in me.

Little by little, I found myself moving away from much of what I was raised to think, feel and believe. Away from home, the opportunity to try new things was tremendous. Pierce my ears (something my overly strict mother frowned upon). Dye my hair? Smoke a cigarette? Yes, yes, and YES!

I would like to say my joining the Air Force was about serving my country or making a difference. After all, military women have performed all sorts of jobs, from code breakers to photographers and a host of others.

The truth is, I went into the Air Force to escape an overly strict childhood and the lack of career prospects. I also went in because of the naysayers: the women who came to my mother's beauty shop and questioned why a nice girl like me wanted to go into the service.

Their horror stories abounded! "My niece went into the Army and came home with a lot of problems," said old Ms. Johnson, a lady with blue hair.

Mrs. Smith knew a lady whose granddaughter went into the Navy and came home with a husband who had been dishonorably discharged, who abused her when he drank.

Consequently, I stayed on active duty the first four years to prove to my mother and those women that I could do it. For the second four years, I did it for myself: travel opportunities, educational benefits, and much more.

Lastly, I stayed in because I finally discovered that the Air Force was not just a job, and it was way more than just an adventure.

Before the military, I'd lived a life unscripted. In truth, the military guided my life's trajectory. The skills honed, time management, the ability to make quick decisions, resolve problems, motivate, and lead others have all been transferrable to my subsequent careers. Likewise, the Air Force inspired fearlessness. Thus, I'm unafraid of changes, be it new ideas, locales, or situations.

Not only did the Air Force provide me the opportunity to travel, but I also experienced things I had never experienced before, like eating octopus tempura which I recently learned didn't have to be tough if you cooked it correctly.

Or like driving through logging standoff where our tour bus was met by men with guns in Panama, as we traveled to visit with several native tribes in the Panamanian jungle.

More than a mere slogan, the Air Force's "Aim High" became my personal mantra. Using the military GI Bill, I obtained not one but two degrees, allowing me to venture into new territory as a leader.

When many people learn that I served for over twenty years, they are surprised. "I can't believe you were in the service, they say. Then, they thank me for my service. "Thanks so much for your kind words," I reply. Still, I chose that life, and I was honored to have served.

MEMORIES BY THE WINDOW

Through my kitchen window, I watched as a robin splashed happily in the birdbath in my back yard, which was now filled to the brim from the torrential downpour from the night before.

Birds constantly fill my backyard with their melodious song. Squirrels also flock to my yard, their movements fraught with hunting for food. All of them provide me with hours of entertainment and enjoyment.

In my bright, cozy kitchen with its buttercream walls, in my mind's eye, I see my mother, long gone, in this very same pose. With an apron tied over her Sunday-go-to-meeting dress, she prepared meals for her two

Nubian princesses — from food scraps, imagination, and love.

Gazing through window panes so clean the glass appeared invisible to the naked eye, I remembered wondering what she saw.

Was she seeing herself as a child, the oldest of eight, forced into adulthood far too soon? A child, like so many others back then, with a sickly mother and a stern father, struggling to feed his brood from the puny fare, the result of an unforgiving patch of red clay on their family's small farm?

As a young girl, had she just once longed to play dress-up? To smear red-hot candies across her lips like lipstick before popping them into her mouth instead of combing her four younger sisters' long thick hair?

Instead, she found herself washing and ironing the family's clothes. Found herself performing the back-breaking task of planting straight rows of seeds into freshly turned earth.

Followed by the tedious tasks of watering and weeding tender plants, instead of hanging out with friends, she went to bed early and got up early to get her sisters and brothers off to school, only to return home to start everything all over again.

Or, perhaps like me, she was simply enjoying the antics of the birds or the flowers that she planted each spring. I still fondly remember the marigolds and zinnias resplendent in vibrant technicolor standing tall in the warm southern sun. And, who could forget the rooster combs with their scarlet tops swaying gently in the breeze?

Soon, a blue jay joined the robin. A cardinal soon joined them. First drinking, they splashed happily about in the water, flecking it on the flowers at the base of the birdbath. At the threatening appearance of five large crow-like birds, the others flew away as quickly as they had appeared. Watching them a few minutes longer, I was suddenly snapped back into the present as the phone rang.

Reaching for it, I told myself that I would only talk with whoever it was for a few minutes, as the need to run outside and empty water from the birdbath was urgent. Although it made a refreshing fountain and swimming pool for the birds, a birdbath full of water had been known to breed mosquitoes that breed disease.

It turned out that the phone call was from my sister, who said she too could only talk for a few minutes. She shared that she was thinking of me as she too gazed out her kitchen window, miles away in Virginia. She, too, remembered our mother doing the same. Speaking for a few minutes, she promised to call again soon, when she had more time to talk.

Ending the call by telling each other that she was loved, I headed for the backyard. The birds were all gone. I was glad as the big blackbirds can be scary.

A shudder escaped me as I recalled their violence in the 1963 movie, The Birds, where, for some reason, they viciously attacked the townspeople.

As I emptied the birdbath, my mind flashed back to something I learned a long time ago. In life, you frequently have to take the bitter with the sweet. And that nothing lasted forever.

Hand Over The Chocolate, And No One Gets Hurt

When I was a young girl, all the women in my "village" seemingly carried some kind of mint, chewing gum, or candy in their purses. More often than not, the candy was some kind of peppermint that came in various shapes.

For example, a small candy cane would be broken into pieces to share with children and adults. And it was common that a lady would ask another if she had a stick of gum or a mint. It also wasn't unusual for someone to break a piece of gum in half and give a piece to someone else.

Alas, more times than I care to mention, I think some older women confused candy with medicine by offering Horehound candy drops. Googling Horehound candy, I discovered it was typically used for digestion and other things.

Light brown in color, the taste hinted at licorice, sugar, and some mystery ingredient. Tar, maybe? You know, like the stuff used to fix streets. Chocolate would have been my preference.

On second thought, chocolate probably would not have done well, hanging out in the bottom of those purses, as more than likely, a Hershey bar or Kit Kat would have become a melty mess.

In truth, chocolate plays a huge role in our lives. So much so that there are a number of books written about the subject. A while back, I came across a cute little book entitled *Hand Over the Chocolate, And No One Gets Hurt.*

Frankly, I can relate. Unlike some men, chocolate has been there for us women in many crises. For example, we reach for a Kit Kat or Snickers bar at the first sign of PMS and other women's issues.

Depending on the crisis, we often also reach for a bag of potato chips to go along with the chocolate. Long for a little kiss, and there is no guy around? Reach for one comprised of chocolate. Yes, there truly are times when chocolate can solve a problem.

Big on education, my mother often took my sister and me to museums and other places where we could learn and experience different things.

Once, we went to an Amish farm. I think my mother wanted us to see that folks did not actually *die* from doing chores as I once thought (and must have crazily uttered out loud).

Another time, we visited Hershey, Pennsylvania, the birthplace of chocolate. Man, chocolate was everywhere, as far as our eyes could see

There were a number of machines that rapidly dispensed chocolate pieces and packaged them. Full disclosure, I did not see any women stuffing chocolate into their bras like in that old *I Love Lucy* episode.

Granted, the bliss generated as a piece of chocolate slowly melts on one's tongue is short-lived. However, with so much going on in the world these days, I tend to find peace wherever peace can be found.

Just yesterday, I found it for a few minutes. Those few minutes were the time it took to eat a Hershey bar with almonds.

The Tale Of The Bait That Got Away

All the women's magazines I read back when my husband Ronnie and I were first dating claimed that the way to a man's heart was not by way of his stomach (not as old wives' tales had led us to believe), but by showing an interest in what he liked.

Meeting when the two of us were stationed at Mountain Home Air Force base in Idaho, on our 4th date, Ronnie invited me to go fishing. I should have seen it coming when he advised me to wear my combat boots.

It was a beautiful Idaho day. As far as the eye could see, the Snake River picked up the color of the sky as it reflected like a mirror on the water's surface. Indeed, it was a perfect way to spend time alone with someone I was growing to care for.

"You are really going to like fishing," Ronnie promised as we drove several miles away from the base. "Where we are going, you can actually see the fish jump out of the water," he added.

After driving for some time, we turned onto an unpaved road. Even though I had easily marched five miles in my combat boots throughout military basic training, walking what seemed like that amount on hard, uneven rocks left me tired.

"We'll stop here," he finally announced. Walking down to the water's edge, he stood overlooking the calm water.

"If the fish aren't biting here, we'll move farther down, okay?" He asked.

Opening one of two containers of squiggly worms, he bent down to bait two fishing poles. Spotting two huge boulders next to each other, I immediately sat down on one. Suddenly, something black slithered between the boulders where I sat.

"Snake!" I screamed, scrambling to get up and banging my hip on the other boulder.

"Honey, you are scaring the fish," my handsome fisherman warned.

"I don't see any fish, but I did see a snake," I remarked, searching to see where it went.

Sticking two fishing poles into the mud, he unfolded two small folding stools, where I sat so close to him that he could barely bait his hooks. Opening a soda for him and one for me, I kept my eyes on my surroundings.

Slithering creatures aside, the truth was I found fishing to be a peaceful outing. Quite frankly, it was a nice way to get away from the rigors of the base with its 24/7 alerts, its 12-hour shifts, and the loud rumble of planes departing and returning to the base flight line.

Suddenly an idea hit me. While Ronnie sat patiently waiting for the fish to attack his poles, I dumped a few worms out of the container when he was not looking, covering them up with dirt. There was a method to my madness: As I thought we could leave once he ran out of bait.

A couple of hours later, as he draped three good-sized trout along the water's edge, he remarked, "I didn't realize that I had used so much bait." Stooping down, he opened the second container and rebated his poles.

Periodically, I again dumped out more of the bait. Six fish later, he baited his poles for the last time.

"You about ready to go, honey?" He asked.

"Whenever you are," I replied. Underneath my breath, I uttered that I had been ready to go as soon as I saw the snake.

Back in the barracks, I spied those stupid magazines that I read about men and what they liked. Ripping them up, I hurled them into the trash.

Later, recounting my day with my dorm mates and how I had tossed out the bait, I looked up and saw Ronnie standing in the doorway of our dorm's dayroom.

"So that's what happened with my bait? I didn't think I had used it up that quickly," he said.

We have all heard the fish stories of the "big one" that got away, but did you ever hear the one about the bait that did?

Channeling Scarlet O'Hara, on Our Forty-Third Anniversary

On a balmy day in March, Ronnie and I pulled up to Twelve Oaks, the once private home turned bed and breakfast. The occasion? Our 43rd anniversary.

Ronnie, recuperating from another health episode and my not wanting to venture too far from home to celebrate, I turned to my BFF, Google. Typing in such search words as "no more than one to two hours away." "Romantic and unique" had led us here.

Inspired by the film *Gone with the Wind* glancing around, I was immediately transported to what it must have been like during Scarlett O'Hara's day.

Except for the charging ports for electric cars, next to the spot where we parked our Jaguar, the plantation house and lavish grounds invoked flashbacks of another period in time.

Located in Covington, Georgia, Twelve Oaks was built in 1836. At 10,000-square-feet, it had 12 bedrooms and 12.5 bathrooms. Besides the numerous themed rooms, it also featured a formal parlor and a number of other formal rooms. Letting ourselves in, I immediately felt at home.

Due to the newly creaking of my knees, where each competed to see which one squeaked the loudest (it's the left one, in case anyone is interested), we bypassed the rooms upstairs, which required navigating the grand staircase, choosing the "Frankly Scarlett Junior Suite," located on the first floor.

For a romantic like me, whose heart flutters at the sight of a luxurious canopy bed, our room was reminiscent of bygone days, seamlessly combining nostalgic ambiance with modern appeal.

"Do you like it?" I asked my husband upon entering it.

"Yes, it's very nice, baby." He replied, spotting the 55″ flat panel television. Taking off his shoes, he immediately sprawled across the bed, which creaked under his weight.

As I surveyed the in-suite bathroom, with its huge shower that included multiple rain shower heads, plus a hand spray, I envisioned kids running through sprinklers on a hot day. I could not wait until Ronnie and I tried it.

Through the shuttered windows, the front porch with its massive columns beckoned. Grabbing the book I bought with me, I headed outside.

On the quiet porch, it was easy to imagine Scarlett O'Hara sitting there, her full skirts spread out around her, sipping lemonade or a Mint Julip.

There, I exhaled for the first time since my husband's carotid artery surgery. Married without children and with no family in the area, waiting in the 'Famil' Waiting Room at Emory University Hospital scared and alone, was now a distant memory.

Channeling Scarlet, tucked in the comfy bed, we slept until breakfast. In the formal breakfast room, we chatted with the other guests.

Some, like us, were there simply to unwind. Others wanted to revisit history or soak up the movies and

TV vibes of those filmed at Twelve Oaks and the surrounding small town.

As my mind touched on that place inside me where fear about my husband's health constantly lived, Twelve Oaks was just what we both needed. Could I have selected a better place to celebrate 43 years of love? Frankly, my dear, I do not believe I could.

My Temporary Disability Gave Me An Appreciation For Those with Permanent Ones

"It's going to get cold," I told my husband. Reaching for his cell phone, he tapped the weather app.

"The temperature is 72 degrees," he says, looking at me oddly.

"I don't care; the temperature is about to drop," I replied stubbornly.

Was I some kind of *weather whisperer*? No, however, since my accident, I have recognized any pending changes in the weather.

It has been said that accidents frequently happen in the home. It's true. Mine happened as I attempted to walk around the family cat, who, for some reason known only to him, decided to sprawl on the rug in the upstairs foyer.

As I approached the stairs, he jumped up, startling me. Attempting to break my fall, I grabbed hold of the banister on the left of the steps, coming down funny on my right ankle.

Hearing the noise, my husband rushed to see what was happening. Seeing me, he asked, "Are you all right? Did you fall?" Typically a quiet man, questions rolled off his tongue.

When I tried to stand and put weight on my leg, pain shut through it. With Ronnie's help and hopping on my good leg, I limped toward the bed. There, we noticed my ankle had started to swell.

"You need to go to the hospital," he said. Helping me to the car, we headed to the emergency room. Employed at Emory University hospital the past few years at that time, he took me there.

X-rays showed that I had fractured my ankle. Due to the way I had fractured it, my ankle required surgery, where a non-weight bearing screw was inserted through my entire ankle to keep the bone steady while it healed.

So as not to fall and permanently injure my ankle, for four weeks, the only way my doctor would allow me to go to work or move around was by wheelchair.

Throughout my recovery, I got a small taste of what disabled people experience daily. Before my injury, I never realized how heavy many doors were or how often people failed to hold them for me when I was using the wheelchair and crutches. Perhaps they thought it best to simply get out of my way?

While temporary, my physical disability revealed how difficult it is to navigate life with physical challenges. And doing so with a smile, especially on days when even smiling, hurts.

ODE TO GOOD GIRLS

For as long as I can remember growing up, I was encouraged to be a "good girl." As I understood it, good girls were expected to dress and act a certain way. There were also a lot of things that good girls did not do.

They did not wear clothing that drew unwanted attention to them. They did not pierce their ears or anything else on their bodies. Good girls did not crack gum, wear red clothing, or wear white after Labor Day. In my opinion, good girls did not seem to have much fun.

As such, all I could think about were ways to be *bad*. Not so bad that I would be forced to wear an orange jumpsuit, but the *bad* where big earrings dangled from my pierced ears. The type of bad that allowed a ponytail to swing from side to side whenever I walked.

I wanted to be the girl that the "fly girls/cool girls" looked up and modeled themselves after, the girl that all the cool boys wanted to date. I longed for a leather coat because, you know, leather coats were *cool*.

My mother would not hear any of it. I was going to be a good girl if she had anything to do with it, and that was that.

Many of us continue to carry the "good girl" mandates around with us. For instance, we often walk on eggshells in relationships to avoid offending others. Sometimes it even affects our intimate relationships.

"You want me to do what?" We ask. "I don't think the chandelier folks had that in mind when they created them! But, you know, maybe we could try it."

At some point, we need to stop worrying about others' feelings about how we live our lives. Full disclosure: this did not happen for me until I ran away from home to join the military.

First, I got my ears pierced. Then I got a double piercing in one ear and three in another, just because. Twenty years ago, at age 50, I got my first leather coat.

Today, I own three leather jackets and a long leather trench coat. And yes, the smell of leather and the feeling of owning and wearing one is exactly how I imagined.

I frequently chew gum and even crack it. I frequently wear white after Labor Day. In Atlanta, no one even appears to notice or even care.

I also own a red dress, a pair of red heels, and a pair of red boots. They look good to me. The truth is, frankly, I feel a little naughty whenever I wear my dress, shoes, and boots. I am neither a good girl nor a bad one, just a girl finally living life on my terms.

STRONG WOMEN

One day it dawned on me that my journey into womanhood was born on the shoulders of many strong women. Thus, whenever life throws me a curveball—as life is so often prone to do, or whenever I'm retaining water and my Spanx threatens to cut off circulation to my entire lower region—I am reminded of those women who suffered more severe afflictions.

I am the product of a woman born of ancestors who retrieved from the earth remedies for everything that ailed me—from colds to sweaty feet. (Do not act like you never heard of things like sassafras and similar herbs.) From her, I learned to use my imagination to "make do" with whatever was handy or needed to be done.

In my veins also flows the blood of women with black history in their heads: women who regaled me with stories about women like Madame CJ Walker, who turned dressing women's hair into a mega business, proving that women could be both entrepreneurial and financially solvent.

Within my "village" was a slew of play 'aunties' and other women who cried tears of joy as each of my birthdays came and went, as I dodged the bullet of teenage pregnancy and sidestepped the drug boogeyman.

Inside me lives the spirit of women who, while not slaves to fashion, were trendsetters in their own right. Standing proudly in their jaunty hats and hand-me-down dresses often re-stitched by hand to fit them, these women sewed enough seeds of wisdom and decorum in me to last a lifetime.

Resplendent in their recycled garments, they reinforced a life-long message that clothes do not make the man or woman: that it's what is inside you, and not some designer's label, that binds the fabric of a person's life.

Modern Sojourners, these women learned first-hand that being a woman was not easy. Some were women alone by choice, others by death or other happenstance. Unfortunately, some remained with men who saw them as bandages for their own wounds. Thinking it was better than being alone.

These women realized too late that what the elders proclaimed was true: "If you make your bed hard, you have to lay in it." With one hand on the Bible and the other raised toward the heavens, they stayed and laid in the hard beds they made.

As I reflect on my life's accomplishments, I am indebted to all these women who, individually and collectively, nurtured me.

Today I frequently find myself surrounded by women of extraordinary character and strength, such as the scores of women struggling to raise a male child alone in a world where daily young black males live in fear of those around them.

Sadly, their lectures to their sons will not only be about respecting women and themselves but also how they should act if the police ever stops them. While police are supposed to "protect and serve" all people, this is not always the case.

So, it is to these women that I pay homage, even on days when I stumble and sometimes even fall from the weight on my shoulders called life.

Instead, I get up, dust myself off, and forge ahead because daily, I see those women in my mind's eye. Those courageous women whose unselfishness helped me become the person I am today. Those proud women, those brave women, those strong women.

My Guardian Angel

(An Angel Helped My Husband Save My Life)

I grew up hearing about diabetes from family members diagnosed with it. My paternal grandfather had had it, and so did my favorite uncle. One of my aunts was diagnosed with it in her late 50s. A diagnosis at that age is often referred to as "late-onset" diabetes.

Those that had it described it as having "the sugar." Others called it "sugar diabetes." Those that had it also claimed it came from eating too much candy and too many desserts. As I loved a great dessert, I knew I would get it; I just knew it!

However, when diabetes came, it arrived with a vengeance. My husband Ronnie and I had just approached the rental car booth in Rapid City, South Dakota when suddenly I realized that my mouth had gone absolutely dry. Bone dry, like no moisture. None!

Unbeknownst to me, my blood glucose was creeping steadily upward throughout the weekend. Extreme thirst, frequent trips to the restroom, and total exhaustion competed with the excitement of my undergrad college's annual homecoming activities, where I received the school's Alumni Special Achievement Award for empowering women and girls through my mentorship, books, and other writings.

Returning home to Atlanta, Ronnie took me to the nearest emergency room, where I learned that my blood glucose had risen to over 900. (A normal blood sugar is typically below 140 upon waking.) There, I received my prognosis, Type 2 diabetes. I was 57, around the same age as my aunt, when she was diagnosed.

In the hospital, an IV in each arm slowly lowered my dangerously high blood sugar. Where I slept beneath the tangle of tubes and wires, oblivious to everything around me.

Throughout my entire hospital stay, my doctor and all the nurses told me I was lucky I was not in a diabetic coma or *worse*. Hearing this, I broke down and cried. A retired, decorated Air Force vet, I seldom cried.

It took four days to lower my blood glucose to reach a safe range. As high blood sugar affects the eyes, among other organs, it took a lot longer for my vision to clear.

After four days, I was finally discharged from the hospital, but not before a diabetic counselor taught me how to inject myself with insulin. "The trick is to pinch a little fat on your stomach and then inject yourself," she said.

Thank goodness this fat on my stomach is good for something, I thought. Still, if someone had told me that a girl who hated needles could inject herself without passing out, I would not have believed it.

Back home, admittedly, I hosted a pity party for one, complete with a party hat. Then, I got busy learning to adjust to my "new normal." Two days after returning home, I got up and took my shot. The last thing I remember was sitting on the couch in my family room.

Suddenly, a woman appeared before me. My first thought was that she had kind eyes. Stretching her hand toward mine, she said, "Come with me. We need to find Ronnie, and quickly." Upstairs, Ronnie, my husband of thirty-six years at the time, was watching football.

I came to, sitting on the steps in my foyer, where two paramedics stood over me. Looking frightened, Ronnie explained that I had just been released from the hospital for diabetes.

Pricking my finger, one paramedic read the glucometer's reading: 69! Much like super high blood glucose, super low numbers can cause a person to fall into a coma or worse.

"Do you have any peanut butter?" One paramedic asked.

"Are you allergic to peanuts, madam?" The other paramedic rapidly fired questions at me. Shaking my head no, he looked to my husband for confirmation.

"Can you make her a peanut butter and jelly sandwich, and quickly?" The EMT asked my husband, who rushed to do this.

As I slowly ate, one of the paramedics asked if I wanted to go back to the hospital. Again, shaking my head no, they left.

"What happened? I asked Ronnie, still feeling a little shaky. "How did I get here in the foyer?"

"Something told me to check on you," He said. "As I came down the stairs, you were headed up the stairs toward the kitchen." (Past the kitchen was my foyer.)

"I called your name, but you didn't answer; you just kept walking. You also had your hand stretched oddly at your side like you were holding hands with someone." He added, looking at me strangely.

"You scared me to death!" He continued. "I pondered whether to call EMS or take you to the nearest hospital myself."

Still visibly shaken, he added, "Had I driven you to the hospital, you might not have made it." Even now, the thought of losing her shook him to the core.

Holding tightly to each other, I realized that the kind-eyed lady must have been an angel. I always believed that angels helped you when you needed it. Looking skyward, I whispered, "Thank you for helping Ronnie to save my life."

A Seasoned Woman

Some time ago, I realized that I had become what author Gail Sheehy had once coined a "seasoned woman" in her book of the same name. To tell the truth, when I think of anything seasoned, thoughts of stuff sprinkled with salt and pepper spring to mind. Oh, we cannot forget onion, onion powder, garlic, and seasoned salt. Somehow, this was not how I viewed myself as a woman.

Further reading on the subject, I learned that a "seasoned woman," according to Sheehy, was a woman who had been "marinated" in life experiences. Okay, that was better.

Combined with many flavors—spicy, tart, and sweet —the seasoned woman has supposedly shrugged off society's morals, along with its dictates about who she should be, to finally realize who she was.

Sheehy also explained that the seasoned woman is someone in their 50s or older, finally coming into their own, even reinventing themselves. Okay, now she was talking about me, I thought.

Unlike my predecessors, who thought it was unseemly for a woman to tell her age, as a seasoned woman, I am thrilled to tell folks my age, taking enormous pleasure when they tell me that I don't look it.

I admit to enjoying both the AARP magazine and Bulletin that appears in my mailbox, secretly happy that it is addressed to my husband and not me.

Admittedly, this seasoned thing is kind of complex. For example, when going to Walgreens to pick up my hypertension medication, I also purchase personal lubricant, breath mints (fresh breath is important), and frosted green nail polish.

When visiting the beauty salon to have blondish streaks applied to hide my few gray hairs, I am often the only woman there wearing cobalt blue polish tipped with gold on my toenails and sporting an arm full of colorful bangles. Did I hear you say, "Go 'head on, diva?"

More importantly, being a seasoned woman also entitled me to question stuff. Like why aren't there more sexy shoes for women my age that look cute on my feet but won't throw my back out while walking?

Or why, after a certain age, does gray hair appear on your body in the strangest places like your chin, eyebrows, and nostrils? Yes, recently, there was one even there.

It is true: becoming a seasoned woman has given me wings. Subsequently, I have begun to take risks. For instance, I recently tore the tag off of a pillow. Nothing happened!

Yes, I have finally become the woman I was destined to be. A little spicy, kind of sweet, and sometimes, even a little tart, when I need to be.

IF YOU GIVE SOMEONE A FALSE NAME, TRY TO REMEMBER WHAT IT IS

As a long-time mentor of young men and women, I frequently get asked tough questions. For instance, some time ago, one of my young women asked me what I thought about online dating.

Actively seeking 'Mr. Right,' she frequently found herself dating both Mr. Right Now and Mr. Wrong, who in her defense favored Denzel Washington. Alas, her most recent date had been with Mr. Crazy, whom she failed to recognize until the stalking began.

First, I reminded her that I might not be the right one to ask about dating. Married for over forty-eight years to the same man, it had been a long time since I dated. I suspect this comes as a great relief to Ronnie).

I told her that with her past dating experience, dating someone online could not be much worse. I also shared that I came from a generation where women often played many games when it came to dating, something I never really understood, but I regress.

One of those games was giving a guy fake names and fake phone numbers. Of course, it would not be right if I did not have a unique story/experience to highlight my point.

Like the time, many years ago when my then BFF and I took a trip to Las Vegas.

We had just left one of the casinos and headed to another when this guy rode up to us on skates—yes, skates. Frankly, since I never learned how to skate, I was a mite jealous. Then I thought, a grown man skating on the streets of Las Vegas: that is just plain weird!

Anyway, "Skate Man" approached us, asking where we were going. Sheri, not her real name, answered, so I did not bother. Frankly, I was more interested in trying my hand at another slot machine.

Of course, it was as hot as you know what outside, and I longed to get back into a cool building and get something cool to drink: preferably a Screw Driver or Tom Collins, do not judge me!

"So, what are your names?" Skate Man asked. I confess I was tempted to give him a false name. Again, Sheri answered for the both of us, telling him that her name was Mary. Mary? Seriously? I don't recall what she told him mine was.

Skate Man kept up a running commentary—about what I have no clue—while skating around us the entire time. I guess one does not stand still when wearing skates.

Getting hotter and thirstier by the minute, I decided that we needed to cut this confab short. So I asked, "Mary, are you about ready to go?" No answer. Sheri/Mary kept chatting.

A little louder, I asked, "Mary, are you about ready to go?" Again, nothing. Finally, I asked much louder, "MARY, are you about ready?"

Sheri/Mary had forgotten her name before suddenly remembering with my increased volume. Bidding Skate Man goodbye, we left him skating to his next encounter, I suppose.

The lesson here? If you give someone a false name, it helps to remember it. To be honest, I probably would have forgotten it too. That is why I do not play games, give folks false information, or talk to men on skates.

As to my thoughts on online dating, I reminded my mentee that being careful should be her main objective. If someone seems to be too good to be true, proceed slowly.

Lastly, put them in check right then and there if they show you a part of their body you did not ask to see (I am told that happens a lot online).

After all, we are modern women: we are not ashamed to ask if we want to see that. This last tip should be considered whether dating in person or online.

A Letter to My Husband:

(About My Fear And Anxiety Of His Driving While Black)

Dear Ronnie,

I never used to be afraid. I have felt anxious about pop quizzes in school or having enough money to pay my bills as a young adult. Will you still love me once my "brickhouse" figure has morphed into a mansion — complete with a carport?

Then, suddenly, the vows "in sickness and in health" raised their ugly head. "Myocardial infarction," the doctor said. A "heart attack," he clarified, noticing my confused expression. Through the years, one health crisis after another has been your constant companion.

Anticipating possible catastrophes, I created a verbal checklist for you. Are you wearing your medical ID bracelet announcing you have a chest defibrillator and are diabetic? These are critically important whenever you go out without me.

Do you have your cell phone? Did you put your dental bridgework in? Are you wearing clean underwear? Okay, the last two are for vanity's sake — mine! The last is a throwback from my mother's "make sure you are wearing clean underwear in case you are ever in an accident" mantra.

Still, there are those things I cannot prepare for that frighten me the most. Such as when you, a Black man, leaves the house alone. My fear when you have been gone too long (or seems like it) simmers much like a pot of water.

Although you arrived home safely that day, it does not mean the fear has ended; it just ended for that particular day. The truth is, this debilitating fear never ends.

Alas, the incident I once feared has already occurred. The one where you had been stopped for "driving while Black" when returning home from a guys' night out.

"Have you been drinking, sir?" you said the policeman asked as he approached your car.

You, a retired military veteran with a second career at a prestigious Atlanta hospital, told him the truth. You admitted to having one beer to be sociable. "I don't really like beer, so I did not finish it," you said.

"While you are not under arrest or anything, I don't think you should drive. It's for your safety," the officer added.

"Do you have someone you can call to come get you?" (Incidentally, my husband does not remember learning why he was stopped in the first place). Could it have been because he had been driving a brand new car at that time?

This was before cellphones, so my fear was when the police officer called me to come to pick you up. Adding that you were not under arrest but that it was for your safety did nothing to stifle my fear even a little bit.

Shaking, I called my sister. "Can you come to pick me up?" I quickly explained what little I knew.

Living close by, and with her sleeping toddler bundled into his car seat, she picked me up and dropped me off where you were parked in a nearby school's parking lot.

Although that particular incident turned out alright, it still shook us up. Once back home, I burst into tears. A decorated Air Force airman, a warrior, I seldom cry.

The possibility that this incident could be repeated and could turn deadly, wars with my constant worry right up there with your health.

Yes, I know my reminding you what to do if you are ever stopped by the police as if you were a child irritates you. However, it could save your life.

So, baby, please do what the policeman says. Do not make any sudden moves, and keep your hands where they can be seen at all times. After all, you can only seek resolution for any perceived injustices if you are still alive to do so.

Lastly, please keep your insurance and registration handy. Keep your speed under the limit. And please, please, do not ever drink and drive.

Altercations with police blasted all over television these days are grim reminders to wives like me and why I fear for you. Hearing Eric Garner gasping, "I can't breathe!" due to the police chokehold resulting in his death left me horrified. Much like the turbulent 60s, once again, our lives and our love are overshadowed by fear.

I get it: cops are scared and, rightly so. Still, could that fear result in the worst possible scenario imagined: the killing of our Black men and boys?

Alas, the answer is yes. Too often, claims of self-defense are actually something more insidious —hatred.

Query. When did the lives of Black males in our society become so insignificant? Not even my degrees in Sociology, Psychology, and a Master's in researching the human condition helps me understand why after being stopped for a broken taillight and reaching for his license and registration at the officer's request, Philando Castile was shot four times.

How does this happen in a so-called "civilized" society? In the 21st century? Maybe author William Faulkner was right when he wrote, "The past is never dead; it's not even past."

When will it all end? When will we see the end to "being Black in the wrong place" as Castile's mother tearfully lamented upon learning her son had been shot and killed?

Yes, Black lives matter. All lives matter. The sad truth is, we Black women know the fear of losing our sons, lovers, or husbands better than any other woman in the world.

Love,

"Peaches" (his pet name for me)

You Deserve Good Things

You are blessed with strength!

Within you is a wellspring of love,
hope, and faith, that gives you the courage to spare.

Enough to share,
and enough to see you, and yours through and
beyond any difficulty.

Yes, you may be facing challenges.
But *you* are absolutely more powerful than *they* are.

Woman's World
6/8/20[1]

---

1. "You Deserve Good Things." Women's World 8 June 2020.
   Print.

I'll Dance, So Please Somebody Ask Me

Growing up, my mother was really strict. She did not smoke or drink, except for enjoying a taste of this really sweet wine called Manischewitz. I, too, did not drink or learn how to smoke until I left home for the military.

My mother also did not approve of dancing. Her one exception was the waltz, which she considered a graceful dance. All others, like The Twist, the Mashed Potato, and other dances popular back then she thought would throw a person's back out.

In elementary school, we learned how to do the waltz. Because my class had more girls than boys, a few of us had to dance with another girl. I remember thinking I would probably never dance the waltz when I grew up, the same way I thought I would probably never use some of the other stuff we were taught in school.

Admittedly, my "Mashed Potato" skills looked more like I was having some kind of fit. However, I really liked The Twist. In fact, it was one of the few dances I felt I was really good at. Of course, I only did it whenever my mother was out of the house.

Today, I find myself dancing as often as I can. Usually, it is around the house. While listening to "ole school" with my stereo speakers turned up *loud,* I 'bust dust bunnies' with a feather duster, while I also 'bust a move.'

Not only does dancing make me feel alive, it makes me feel free. It also makes me feel a little naughty. Knowing that my mother would disapprove causes me to dance with wild abandonment.

A Moment For You

You have so much to give, and you give so much!
Spot-on insights and sound advice,
great ideas, and creative solutions,
a shoulder to cry on, and a helping hand.
You've got it all, and you're always on call!
Part angel, part cheerleader, and part coach:
It's no wonder so many give thanks to you.

Woman's World Magazine
9/14/20[1]

---

1. "A Moment For You." Women's World 14 September 2020.
Print.

CONSIDER THE SOURCE

Have you ever known someone who cannot wait to give you advice on whatever ails you? Alright, I admit that I tend to be one of those people. Every affliction someone has—headache, toothache, toenail fungus —so-called remedies flow from my mouth, like water from a faucet.

I used to think it was a "woman's thing," but I have a male doctor friend who also suggests remedies supposedly "tried and true." Because he is a well-regarded physician, I tend to try many of them.

Admittedly, many of these old-fashioned remedies and other things do work. For example, gargling with warm salt water helps a sore throat better than over-the-counter meds. Mustard does soothe a burn, that is, if you don't mind walking around smelling like a hot dog.

Alas, we have all heeded things that did not work out. For instance, a colleague once shared that she had been gifted a necklace of beads she loved that smelled of Myrrh like the biblical "Frankincense and Myrrh."

She asked if I had ever smelled Myrrh, to which I replied no. I asked my administrative assistant if she had ever smelled Myrrh, to which she also answered no.

I was glad, as I did not wish to appear uncouth, being the only one who had never smelled it.

It spears that over the years, the Myrrh smell had disappeared. So another *friend* suggested that she wet the necklace that perhaps the Myrrh scent would reappear.

Wetting the necklace, much to my colleague's horror, not only did the Myrrh scent *not* return, many of the beads stuck together in a long clump. The good news was once the necklace dried out, she was able to separate it and straighten it out.

Once my administrative assistant and I stopped laughing (sorry), we congratulated our colleague on fixing it. Thus, the moral of this story is to go ahead and try some things. But, before you do, stop for a minute (for instance, ask whether the person knows anything about Myrrh) or the subject in question, then you know, consider the source.

SNEAK PEEK

Select Essays from:

The Venus Chronicles
Diary OF A Fly girl Wannabe
Gilded Pearls
And
Random Notes

Available at Venuschronicles.net Amazon.com, and wherever books are sold online.

Closet Full of Clothes, and Nothing to Wear

From *The Venus Chronicles:*

It starts innocently enough with three little words: "You are invited." As I glance at the words on that ecru-colored card, a metamorphosis occurs. My palms tingle and sweat beads rest on my upper lip.

Words like semi-formal, business casual, or casual elegance swim before my eyes, and I feel lightheaded by the time I get to where I must RSVP.

What the heck is casual elegance anyhow? Is it that long black skirt, the one with the thigh-high split, which I simply had to have the first time that I saw it?

Would it be casually elegant if I wore it with a white silk blouse? Or maybe I could wear that little black dress with my cultured pearls. Surely I could not go wrong with that, could I?

On second thought, maybe I better stay away from black. The last three times I attended an event, I wore black. It started that New Year's Eve when that fine, Denzel Washington lookalike, asked me to dance.

You know, the one who commented that black was a good color for me, as it made me look tall and sexy? However, repeated questions from women friends asking if I was in mourning (you know, wearing black to honor someone deceased) made me realize that maybe I had been wearing too much black lately. Haters!

Perhaps casual elegant was that red knit chemise worn with my red high-heel pumps with the gold tip at the toe that I bought last month. Casually elegant or plain hoochie-mama, I wonder?

According to my mother, nothing quite says vamp or tramp like wearing red from head to toe. Full Disclosure, it's the reason I bought both the dress and shoes in the first place.

What about that navy pantsuit with the mandarin collar and frog button loops? Boring and safe, it screams, versus casual elegance.

In my bedroom, I fling open both closet doors. Like the fashion police, I rifle through the contents, pulling things off hangers and flinging them across the bed along with the clothes I am wearing.

Standing naked in front of a full-length mirror, I stare at my body. Has my butt always been this big? I pondered as I tried on my black skirt.

Pulling out the scale from beneath the bathroom cabinet, I verified that I had not gained any weight. Dang, the dry cleaners must have shrunk my skirt!

Or perhaps the moisture in this house caused the fabric to shrink. (Don't act like you haven't once thought this).

Are my breasts starting to sag? Maybe I need to buy a support bra in black lace with push-up cups? Darn, this white blouse has a stain on it!

Stopping to exhale, I once again peek at my checkbook, then at the calendar. As usual, there is more month left than money.

I give the Anne Klein coat dress and the navy pantsuit a second look with a less critical eye. Both of these could work. Okay, now what about shoes?

Now That I Finally Got My Mind Together, The Rest of Me Is Falling Apart

From *Diary Of A Fly Girl Wannabe:*

As a child, I read everything I could get my hands on, from mysteries to the Bible. From biblical characters like Daniel, who bravely survived the lion's den, I learned that people could survive by using their wits.

Initially, I read literature for great stories and the hours of escapism they provided as I turned page after page. Then, I began to read and even analyze them.

Much like the Little Red Hen, I discovered something. (No, not that constantly looking up to see if the sky is falling can cause whiplash or land you face first in "dog-do." I mean that other lesson.)

"If you want something done right, you usually have to do it yourself." Ask any woman with a husband or children how true this statement is.

From Romeo and Juliet, I learned that a serious "Love Jones" could often be the death of you. However, do not let that stop you from trying to find love.

From Chicken Little, who sometimes was also known as Henny Penny, I learned that we frequently meet a lot of strange folks along the way on life's journey. Hopefully, none with such names as Cocky Locky or Turkey Lurkey. Hey, I am not one to judge.

Socrates, Plato, and Nietzsche were absorbed into my pores like steam in college. Some months later, Jung (a famous psychologist) helped me rediscover my inner child. To tell the truth, until then, I did not even realize that she existed.

Alas, while I have finally got my mind together, the rest of me is going to pot. For starters, there is that one chin hair that persists on growing back even after continued yanking with industrial-strength tweezers.

Lately, it has started playing hardball. Not only was it back, but it had returned with an entourage, all now taking up residence beneath my chin.

Meanwhile, my knees are in competition to see which one of them makes the most noise when I bend over. In case you are wondering, it is the right one. However, I have sworn not to let these things bother me. You see: I am grounded, and I am centered. Finally!

Castor Oil Does Not Cure Everything

From Random Notes:

My mother's answer for everything that ailed us was a good cleaning out. Have a stomach ache? A dose of castor oil purportedly would fix us right up. Got the sniffles, acne, or pigeon toes? Castor Oil, of course!

I suspect we children had the cleanest colon amongst our peers. Granted, this was not anything to break out in song about or cause us to go around high-fiving folks.

For those unfamiliar with Castor Oil, it is a vegetable oil-based laxative obtained from the castor bean or, technically, the castor seed. Colorless or a pale yellow color with no odor but a slightly oily taste, Castor

Oil has been used in everything from soaps to lipsticks. Research indicated that it was used as hydraulic and brake fluids.

While mother swore by castor oil for its colon cleaning principles, I learned others also used it for burns, cuts, and other abrasions. It was also often used to ease headaches: it was certainly used whenever my sister and I reported having one.

Using my new best friend Google, I recently learned that the Castor seed contained Ricin, a toxic protein. (And you all thought I was being paranoid when I once claimed that my mother tried to kill me.) In fact, she tried to do it every fall.

According to Google, even harvesting the Castor seed was not without risk, as allergenic compounds found on the plant's surface could cause permanent nerve damage. Also, according to Google, under the regime of Mussolini, Castor Oil was used as an instrument of intimidation to discourage civilians and soldiers alike from calling in sick either in the factories or in the military.

Castor Oil had the same effect on my sister and me back in the day. We learned from prior experiences to mask stomach aches, runny noses, and hangnails. We truly had to believe that we were on death's door before admitting we were sick because we knew what was coming.

Talk about cruel and unusual punishment! Once, I was given a dose of Castor Oil for simply complaining that my sister was getting on my nerves. First, my mother informed me that I was too young to have nerves. How old did you have to be? I wondered.

After all, according to her, all I had to do was go to school: I did not have to work or worry about making ends meet. Nor did I have to wonder where my next meat and bread were coming from, nor worry about keeping a roof over all of our heads as she did. Still, she gave me a dose of Castor Oil for good measure. I never had nerves again.

One Person's Trash, Etc., Etc.

From Gilded Pearls:

Okay, I admit it: I have a penchant for "found" things. You know, stuff found by the side of the road. That someone put out by the trash. In truth, these items beg me to stop and peruse.

Honestly, the thought of rummaging through other people's castoffs makes me feel a little "dirty," but everything in life is my muse. Alas, my little "hobby" mortifies my husband, so I have learned to go on these little jaunts by myself.

Hopped up on caffeine, my imagination runs wild. For example, that discarded wicker basket would be perfect for my cloth dinner napkins.

An old White Owl cigar box with lid intact cried out to be decoupaged with some Victorian paper decorated with cherubs. An ornate button, hot-glued on for a handle, would make it the perfect place to corral my makeup, hairpins, or buttons.

Full disclosure: there have been items I've collected that I had no idea what they were. For instance, that wrought iron two-tier basket-like-thingy with a pole in the center separating the two tiers. With three iron feet curling inward, it stood about three feet off the floor. Can you imagine someone throwing something like that away?

Spray painted gold and topped with a round mirror: another "find" made a great table next to my husband's recliner. That beautiful find resided in several of the military houses we lived in during our 20 years in the Air Force.

Then there was the bench that my neighbor placed out by the curb. I saw it one Saturday morning as my husband and I headed out to run errands.

It reminded me of the two that stood sentry on both sides of a wooden picnic table under the trees in our back yard when I was growing up.

All too familiar with my body language when I spot a treasure, my husband said, "I know what you are thinking, and we are not stopping."

Despite what he said, I had already told myself that I would get it upon my return—I think he knew it too. In my mind's eye, I saw it cleaned up and spray painted green, with a floral cushion. Oh, what a wonderful place to sit with a cup of tea and admire my flowers in the upcoming months.

I could blame this obsession on some affliction. My mother was reared during the Depression, which taught her to be frugal. Thus, she passed the frugal gene down to my sister and me. As such, I see new uses for stuff others often throw away.

Still, after 48 years together, some things are bound to rub off on a person. Case in point, my husband recently bought home a small, wicker birdcage that he purchased for a dollar at a yard sale. (We don't have a bird.)

He said he thought that "I might do something with it; spray paint it or something." As I smiled, two thoughts sprung to mind: you really can teach an old dog new tricks. And, every now and again, you find something worth keeping.

QUESTIONS FOR BOOK CLUBS, DISCUSSION, ETC.

1. When was the last time you had an act of kindness bestowed upon you?
2. What happened, and how did it make you feel?
3. When was the last time you paid an act of kindness forward?
4. How did it make you feel?
5. Share a humorous incident that happened to you.
6. Name something that no one knows about you.
7. Name something you do today that your mother would not have approved.
8. Share your thoughts on an issue that happened today or happened years ago that impacted you.

ABOUT THE AUTHOR

Carol Gee, M.A., a retired, decorated Air Force veteran and retired university administrator, also did a short stint as a mental health counselor. As such, she likens her books and freelance pieces to be much like "therapy without the couch."

Author of four books, including one that shares her love of upcycling/repurposing flea market, thrift, and dollar store items, her work also appears in numerous magazines, both in print and online. She and her lovely husband reside in Stone Mountain, a suburb of Atlanta.